Data in Digital Advertising

Understand the Data Landscape and
Design a Winning Strategy

Dominik Kosorin

Data in Digital Advertising:
    Understand the Data Landscape and Design
    a Winning Strategy
by Dominik Kosorin

Ad Tech Research

www.adtechresearch.com
ISBN: 978-80-907138-0-2

For Zuzana and Samuel

Contents

Acknowledgments

My wife Zuzana, for her unwavering support and encouragement from the initial idea all the way to publishing. Zuzana Neupauerova and Jakub Novotny, who gave me many valuable suggestions that made this book much better. Damien Alzonne, Ali Bohra, Pascale Dray-Rudzki, Brett House, Megan McKenna, Jana Moran, Chris O'Hara, Benjamin Papazoglou, Rakhi M. Patel, Jochen Schlosser, and many others, for their time and amazing input I would not be able to get otherwise. Anezka Hruba Ciglerova, for the world-class book design and layout.

Introduction

A data revolution is under way in digital advertising. For the first time in history, advertisers are able to know and precisely target individuals with personalized messages at scale, across channels, and in real time. True one-on-one marketing has been a dream for a long time, and although we are not quite there yet, the widespread adoption of advertising data has brought us much closer to this goal – in the span of just a few years. No wonder data is possibly the hottest topic in advertising today, and many organizations are embarking on designing their own data strategies.

Data has forever changed digital advertising, and there is no going back. Advertisers are now able to pinpoint and target very granular, relevant audiences with the right messages at the right time. They can easily reach out to their past or potential customers, and conduct sophisticated prospecting campaigns with minimal waste. Increased relevance directly translates into higher campaign ROI, making data usage in advertising a no-brainer. But running an isolated campaign, albeit more efficient than before, is only scratching the surface of what data can accomplish today and in the future. With the right advertising data strategy and tools to implement it, organizations can build deep customer understanding and data-centered capability over time. The choice is clear – outsmart your competition, or be outsmarted.

But how did data suddenly rise to such prominen-ce? One of the key drivers in the rise of advertising data has been the open programmatic ecosystem. In programmatic, each ad impression is traded individually in an auction, allowing data to inform bidding decisions. If a car manufacturer knows that a person who is about to see an ad is in market for a new sedan, it makes sense to bid high and try to win this impression. Without data, that impression would be just like any other. With data, it is extremely valuable.

Data and programmatic are intertwined – programmatic enables the use of data, and data elevates programmatic to a game changing status. Size of the advertising budget no longer determines success. Instead, digital advertisers are starting to compete on access to and management of quality data.

The last several years have also witnessed rapid rise of standalone advertising platforms such as Facebook or Google AdWords, which are also thriving on data. With huge user bases and a high share of users' attention, these platforms have unparalleled access to individual-level data. Advertisers can easily reach their desired audiences at scale, across devices, and in a brand-safe environment. This value proposition has proven to be very compelling, despite often tight control of data flow on these platforms.

Technology has been another contributing factor in the data revolution. Infrastructure is now available to collect and process vast quantities of data in real time, and activate it immediately in advertising. Data management platforms (DMPs) in particular have been instrumental in empowering advertisers and publishers alike. With a DMP, they can take control of their data and turn it into a serious competitive advantage.

The increasing demand for data has led to an explosion of data vendors and exchanges. Hundreds of data providers exist today, with different scale, availability, and of course quality. Making sense of all these options is not an easy task, and careful testing is often required to make sure each data source is indeed contributing positive value. On the data activation front, advertisers can choose from a broad selection of demand-side platforms (DSPs), ad servers, retargeters, analytics tools, and other solutions.

Naturally, swift adoption of data in digital advertising has raised privacy concerns among both the general public as well as regulators. Some of these concerns are justified, and governments as well as industry bodies are racing to bring clear and transparent rules to data collection and management practices. General Data Protection Regulation (GDPR) in the European Union, along with the proposed ePrivacy Regulation, are some of the most impactful laws pertaining to advertising data.

Scope

This book gives an overview of the advertising data ecosystem as it stands towards the end of 2017. Although it is still early days, the data landscape is already very complex. Readers should get a solid understanding of what advertising data is, how it flows in the current ecosystem, which technologies support it, who are the main players, what are the rules of the game, and how to think about developing an advertising data strategy. Although not required, some level of understanding of digital advertising, especially programmatic, is recommended prior to reading this book. My first book, "Introduction to Programmatic Advertising", is a good way to get up to speed.

This book was written mainly with digital advertisers, both large and small, in mind. It aims to help them jumpstart their journey into the world of advertising data, and provide a framework for thinking about this topic. That said, publisher and agency issues are also covered to some extent.

Both the open ecosystem, as well as standalone advertising platforms are tackled in this book from data perspective. Advertising data is always related to real individuals at the end of the day, regardless of their platform or publisher preferences. Ecosystem (and data flow) fragmentation makes things difficult when it comes to achieving the perfect one-on-one marketing dream – but this might be just a momentary inconvenience.

As for geographic scope, this book is not limited to any particular area. Due to their markets' size and digital maturity, readers from the North America and Europe will perhaps find most that can be directly applied to their circumstances (particularly the selection of data vendors and technology providers available). However, the book is intentionally as general as possible, so that broad concepts can be translated globally with ease.

Book structure

This book is divided into eight chapters. It is best to initially read them in order as they tend to build on each other. However, the book is also designed to serve as an easy reference for specific topics later on.

Chapter one answers some of the essential questions about advertising data – what are its sources, how it is created, or what kinds of data exist. It introduces standard industry data classifications based on source, creation methods, categories, and ownership. These classifications serve as mental "building blocks", establishing common terminology and setting the stage for later chapters.

Chapter two introduces the advertising data eco-system. First half of this chapter briefly introduces its main participant types, such as advertisers, data management platforms, standalone advertising platforms, or third-party data vendors and exchanges. Second half is dedicated to the various data transfer methods, understanding of which is critical in practice.

Chapter three outlines targeting options on major standalone advertising platforms. This broad umbrella term encompasses a wide range of complete advertising solutions with varying degree of openness. Targeting data profiles of Facebook/Instagram, Google AdWords, Twitter, Amazon, LinkedIn, eBay, Pinterest, or Snapchat are included.

Chapter four offers an introduction to third-party data providers, and includes a few dozen vendor profiles. Although most operate exclusively in the open ecosystem, some are also integrated into standalone advertising platforms. Vendor selection is non-exhaustive, giving a flavor of the kinds of data that can be purchased.

Chapter five is an introduction to data management platforms (DMPs). General DMP capabilities are discussed here, to provide a good picture of what this key advertising data technology can accomplish.

Chapter six includes profiles of the top global DMP vendors. These include Adform DMP, Adobe Audience Manager, The Adex, Amobee DMP, Google Audience Center 360, Lotame DMP, MediaMath DMP, Neustar IDMP, Nielsen DMP, Oracle BlueKai, Salesforce DMP and Zipline by KBM Group.

Chapter seven covers data privacy and related regulation. Some key advertising data-related laws and industry rules are discussed here, including General Data Protection Regulation (GDPR), ePrivacy Directive and Regulation, Children's Online Privacy Protection Act (COPPA), Health Insurance Portability and Accountability Act (HIPAA), California Online Privacy Protection Act (CalOPPA), as well as the Digital Advertising Alliance (DAA) Self-Regulatory Program.

Chapter eight serves as a guide to designing an advertising data strategy. It ties all of the previous chapters together, and provides a framework for thinking about advertising data. It should help organizations kick-start development of a strong data-centered capability for a long-term success in digital advertising.

Chapter 1
Advertising data 101

Where does advertising data come from? How is it created? What kinds of data exist? And, very importantly, who owns it? In this introductory chapter, we will explore all of these questions with the help of standard industry data classifications. They provide an excellent mental structure and a foundation for more advanced discussion further in this book. We will look at the most common data sources, creation methods, and categories. Data ownership is tackled in this chapter as well.

It is important to mention at this point that advertising data is always tied to an ID (user ID, cookie ID, etc.), typically representing an individual person, a household, a web browser, or a device. It is this connection that gives advertising data its value, as it enables informed, personalized communication with a specific recipient. A single individual would have many different IDs within the ecosystem – separate IDs are often created for each of their devices, web browsers, advertising platforms, and all the various ecosystem players. Although data can be very valuable despite this ID fragmentation, the industry is striving towards uniting users' many separate profiles into more powerful ID graphs. In the meantime, it is a common practice to pair and exchange the various IDs to enable data transfer and activation within the ecosystem.

A quick note on data privacy is in order as well. In general, no personally identifiable information (often abbreviated as PII) is used in digital advertising. PII includes any data that can either alone, or in combination with other data, identify a real person. Data points such as a person's name, address, social security/passport/national ID number, credit card numbers, phone number, or date of birth typically fall under PII[1]. Most platforms, data management platforms in particular, do not even allow storing and processing of such information. If data containing PII is to be used for digital advertising (commonly onboarded from a CRM database for instance), it is first anonymized. Although advertising data is always tied to an ID as described above, this ID is anonymous and cannot be tied back to a specific person.

Data sources

Data used in digital marketing and advertising comes from several distinct sources. Website data is perhaps the most prevalent, but other common sources include mobile apps, ad campaigns, analytics tools, CRM systems, or email. Naturally, this is not a complete list – each ecosystem participant will have access to different data sources, whether first-party or external, modern or more traditional.

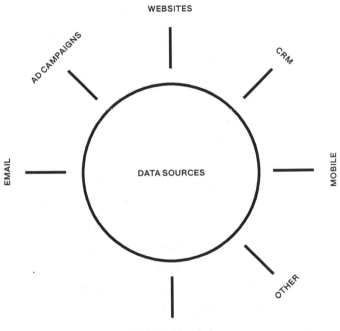

FIGURE 1: COMMON DATA SOURCES

Websites

A large portion of all data used in digital advertising is gathered from websites, as data collection is relatively easy to implement at scale and offers valuable insights into user interest, intent, and characteristics. This data is often collected from owned web properties, or pur- chased from second- or third-parties (defined later). Website data can be grouped into three buckets:

- Content/behavior related
- Declared
- Technical data

As users browse a website, they leave a trace of con- tent and behavioral data signals which can be collect- ed and used. This includes standard signals such as website URL, page title, page keywords, on-site search keywords, page referrer, search keyword used to get to the website, or user ID (e.g. hashed email address) if available. E-commerce websites might include additional signals, like items added to a shopping cart, the prod- uct viewed, the category viewed, or order value. In fact, any user interest, behavior, or characteristic which can be gleaned from their website visit can be turned into a custom data signal. For example, publishers might use semantic analysis to produce high-quality custom signals related to page content (as a proxy for user interest).

Declared data is commonly gathered on websites via registration forms, sweepstakes, questionnaires, web applications, purchase events, or preference settings. If the website uses a login (typical for ecommerce sites, email providers, or social networks, for example), this declared data can be easily linked to a user across their devices and stored over long periods of time.

Technical data relates to devices used to visit a website. Signals include things like web browser, operating system, device or device type (i.e. iPhone 8 vs. cell phone), language, or geo location.

Mobile

When it comes to mobile, there are two common sources of data – mobile apps and mobile websites.

Mobile apps in particular are a treasure trove of behavioral and declared data, as virtually anything a user does with an app can be tracked and paired with their unique advertising ID (IDFA or Identifier for Advertisers on iOS, AAID/GAID or Google Advertising ID on Android). This includes behavioral data points such as app ID, session length, days since the last use, hour of day the app was launched, device resolution, carrier, geo location, actions/events within the app (e.g. purchases, clicks, searches, video plays, social shares, etc.), as well as diagnostic events (such as launches, crashes, upgrades), or number of engaged users in a given time period. Mobile apps are also good for collecting declared data (via forms, preferences, purchases, etc.), as the advertising identifiers on mobile devices are more persistent than cookies.

Mobile websites offer similar data to desktop websites – however, they are much harder to track, as use of third-party and even first-party cookies is restricted on mobile (especially in Safari/iOS, which recently introduced the so-called Intelligent Tracking Prevention).

Ad Campaigns

Ad campaigns are a great source of data, both for advertisers as well as other ecosystem players who might have access to it. Key data signals include impressions, clicks, conversions (such as leads, form submissions, purchases, etc.), and ad interaction events (e.g. exposure duration, ad creative events). Properly tagged, running campaigns should also provide signals such as campaign IDs, creative IDs, business unit IDs, or advertiser IDs.

Analytics Tools

Website analytics tools, such as Google Analytics, are a fantastic source of data on website visitors. They help track on-site measures such as page view duration, the number of pages visited, or visit recency. They can also capture some campaign and website events including impressions, clicks, or conversions of various types. Data gathered with analytics tools can be used for a very granular visitor segmentation – either as a standalone source, or in conjunction with website data obtained by other means.

CRM (Customer Relationship Management) Software

CRM software has been around for a while, and many companies use it to store customer information. Regardless of whether the CRM database is online or offline, data contained within can be brought to digital environment (through a process called onboarding, explained later) and used for online applications such as targeting or analytics. Common CRM data points include customer names, addresses, phone numbers, email addresses, purchase history, contact history, customer segmentation, or loyalty program behavior.

Email data

Email marketing programs (and the related software) can be tapped to provide data for other digital applications.

A typical use case is targeting users via a different channel based on their email marketing behavior (e.g. retargeting someone who unsubscribed from a mailing list with display ads). Email data includes subscription status, engagement behavior (email open rate, click-through rate, etc.), or conversion behavior.

Other data sources

There are many other data sources which can be used for digital marketing and advertising. These range from established sources with offline origins (e.g. public and private records, databases, surveys, or census data), through various panels and point of sale records, all the way to modern, cutting-edge data streams (including for instance wearables, beacons, connected internet-of-things devices, or marketing automation platforms). As long as it can be matched to a digital user profile, digital ID, or device of any kind, any data point can be useful for ad targeting or other applications.

External data

From the perspective of an individual ecosystem player, external data can be seen as a separate source (albeit the provider might have gathered it through some already mentioned means). External data would include any second- or third-party data, as well as data available on standalone advertising platforms.

Data creation methods

When we look at the way data was created, we can distinguish three main groups:

- Declared data
- Inferred data
- Modeled data

Declared data is provided by the users themselves, usually via various registration forms, sweepstakes, and questionnaires. A prime example of declared data owner is Facebook – users not only reveal who their friends and family are (i.e. their social graph), but often fill in their age, gender, or relationship status. Declared data is valuable, as it is usually very close to the truth. Some declared data might be inaccurate though, so it is always good to check if its source is not suspicious (i.e. some online dating sites, chatrooms, etc.).

Inferred data is not given by the users directly, but is deduced – usually from their behavior. If a user is looking at a lot of car reviews, the probability is high that they are in market for a new car. Or if someone reads a lot of photography content, we can assume they are interested in photography.

Finally, modeled data uses a large data set to find users matching a desired profile. Let us say we know a certain characteristic of a seed group – for example their declared gender. An algorithm can look at their other characteristics (or simply related raw data points), and compare these against users of unknown gender. Creating a model, the unknown gender can be estimated (often with very high accuracy). Caution needs to be taken when using modeled data (particularly if purchased from third-party vendors), as quality varies greatly. Results depend not only on the quality of the algorithm used, but also on the data pool (data points included, depth, and breadth), freshness, and reliability of seed data. If possible, it is always a good idea to verify a model against declared data to ensure it is accurate enough.

Data categories

There are several common user-related data categories, including:

- Demographics
- Interest
- Intent

- Lifestyle
- B2B
- Location
- Identity

This grouping usually applies at segment level (i.e. multiple data signals are required for classification), but sometimes can be relevant for raw data signals (e.g. user age or gender). Each data user/vendor might use a slightly different categorization to suit their business or marketing needs.

Demographic and socio-economic data includes characteristics like gender, age, life status (single, married, with children, retired, etc.), wealth, income, financial behavior, or health. This data is often declared by the users themselves, and sometimes modeled to increase scale.

Interest data is typically inferred from user behavior, and often uses weaker but frequent data signals for classification compared to intent data. For example, someone reading a lot of gaming content might be classified as having an interest in computer gaming. Special interest data types include media consumption preferences, seasonal or event-based data, or political inclination.

Similar to interest data, intent data is also commonly derived from user behavior. However, data signals for this classification are typically much stronger, more specific, and sufficiently recent. To illustrate, someone visiting a price comparison site, searching for "PlayStation 4 Pro" and reading several reviews has a very likely intent of purchasing one. While the bulk of intent data is purchase intent, there are other intent sub-categories – such as voting, moving, or service cancellation.

Lifestyle is a broad and relatively vague category, based on clusters of users with similar profiles. Clustering is commonly done in an automated fashion – algorithms are used on pools of raw data to find groups of users similar to each other, but distinct enough from the other groups. These groups (or clusters) are then given descriptions by human analysts to make them usable and marketable. Clustering can be done on general user data (resulting in "Lifestyle" segments, such as "Urban Yuppies" or "Soccer Moms"), or more specific data pools (to create financial, psychographic, or other segmentation).

B2B data tends to be singled out, as it uses specific data sources that are not widely available. B2B data is user-related, focusing on business professionals in their respective roles. Two sub-categories are common – firmographics and B2B intent. Firmographics describe the type of organization a user is working for and their role (industry, size, revenue, function, level, etc.). B2B intent data looks at intent signals in a business context – whether it is business software purchase, renting out office space, or taking out a business loan. Beyond general B2B data, some high-value segments (such as health-care professionals) have their own data segments and providers.

Location data can be used to build unique geo-behavioral segments. These are often based on known locations of points of interest, and users' movement (including dwell time, frequency, etc.) around them. For example, if someone frequently visits shopping malls and spends a lot of time there, they can be classified as an avid shopper. Location segments can be based around activities, intent, or even brand preferences (e.g. loyal Starbucks customer).

Finally, identity data is extremely interesting – its primary use case is building identity graphs of users, their devices, and other related data. To illustrate, an identity data signal might include a combination of cookie ID and hashed email, both related to the same user. By combining many similar signals, a company might be able to build a comprehensive profile of user's cookies, IDs (email addresses, device IDs, etc.) and other identifiers. At scale, an identity graph of millions of users can serve for cross-device/browser/platform ad targeting, frequency capping, measurement, attribution, and other applications.

Data ownership

A common categorization of data used in the digital advertising industry is based on ownership/control, and we can distinguish first-, second-, and third-party data. This distinction is from the perspective of a single ecosystem participant, be it an advertiser, publisher, or an agency.

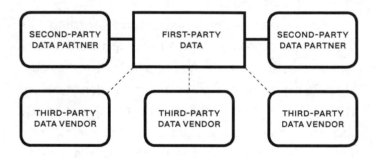

FIGURE 2: DATA CATEGORIZATION BY OWNERSHIP

Each category has its advantages and disadvantages, so it is common to rely on all three when running ad campaigns, analytics, or other applications. Also, availability varies greatly not only by data user (a CPG/FMCG company might have more limited first-party data compared to a large e-commerce site), but also by region or industry.

First-party data

First-party data is collected directly from owned or controlled sources, typically by advertisers or publishers. This is the most valuable, exclusive, and transparent data marketers have – and it is free, apart from the technology cost to make it useful. For example, a publisher can collect data on their visitors – including the content they viewed, the number of visits, or the searches they performed on the site. This data can be used to personalize the website for each visitor, and present content that will be relevant and engaging. This publisher might also choose to sell this data to other parties (typically for ad targeting purposes), opening an additional revenue stream.

As great as first-party data is, limited scale is a major restriction. An advertiser, for instance, can only obtain data on users who actually visit their website, mobile app, or other directly controlled property. Only a fraction of potential customers do so, so other methods have to be used to reach out to the rest. First-party data usage can be also limited due to legal and privacy reasons. In light of GDPR and other regulations, care needs to be taken to obtain user consent and process data in a compliant way.

Second-party data

Second-party data is obtained through partnerships with other entities (typically complementary advertisers or publishers), and is essentially their first-party data. To illustrate, a price comparison site might share their first-party user data with an e-commerce site. To the e-commerce site, this is second-party data. Often, partners would mutually share their first-party data (bilaterally or in a larger co-op) in order to gain a better user understanding, or to increase their cross-device ID recognition. Publisher data co-ops are a common and interesting form of sharing second-party data.

Second-party data has the advantage of a known source and in turn quality, while helping to extend the scale of first-party data. On the downside, each data partnership has to be agreed upon and maintained – which might not be as easy as buying third-party data from external vendors. Privacy regulation is also a major limitation to the use of second-party data, as user consent might often be required – preventing easy ad-hoc data sharing agreements.

Third-party data

Third-party data is obtained from external providers, who have no direct partnership with the buyer. There are hundreds of such data vendors, ranging from global players with a broad selection of audience segments or raw data, to niche local providers. Third-party data is widely available across the ecosystem, and major vendors are directly integrated into DMPs, DSPs, ad servers, and other technologies for easy purchase and activation.

Advantages of third-party data include reach, ease of access, and an increased advertising ROI with good vendors. However, not all vendors offer quality data, and with a proliferation of various offers it is very difficult to uncover data segments that actually bring value. A/B testing and pre-campaign segment analytics can help a lot when evaluating third-party data, and DMPs and DSPs offer tools to make it easier. A whole section of this book is dedicated to third-party data vendors, with brief overviews of a few dozen.

A special case of third-party data is standalone advertising platform data (such as Facebook, Google, Twitter, or Amazon). These large platforms offer a wealth of data for ad targeting, but in general restrict its use to the platform itself. A separate section of this book is dedicated to standalone advertising platform data.

Chapter 2
Data ecosystem

An entire ecosystem has emerged around digital advertising data, driven by development in data collection, usage, and monetization possibilities. Advertisers and agencies create most of the data demand, while publishers, standalone advertising platforms, and third-party vendors/data exchanges provide data supply.

A host of data-related solutions, services, and tools exist to help with various stages of data flow. Data management platforms often serve as central data hubs, aided in data collection by website analytics, onboarding vendors, and tag management solutions. Data activation, especially for ad targeting, is the domain of technologies including demand-side platforms and specialized retargeting vendors, supported by dedicated ad servers and ad measurement solutions.

Finally, due to its sensitive nature, data ecosystem is regulated not only by industry bodies, but increasingly through national and supranational governments. It is clear that the data ecosystem will continue to evolve to meet new opportunities and restrictions, through both consolidation as well as opening of new technology niches. A brief, non-exhaustive overview of the main ecosystem players follows to provide a broad picture. Some of the key players and vendors (such as standalone advertising platforms, data management platforms, and third-party data providers) will be explored in depth in further chapters.

In the second part of this chapter, we will go through common data collection and transfer methodologies. Having learned who participates in the data ecosystem, it will be useful to see which techniques and technologies make data flow.

Advertisers

Advertisers create the bulk of data demand, mainly with ad targeting in mind. With the right data, they can significantly increase advertising return on investment and build very sophisticated, personalized communication strategies. Performance advertisers in particular are heavy users of data, especially if it signals strong intent (popular tactics are keyword-based search advertising or retargeting). Brand advertisers can also take advantage of data (such as user interest or sociodemography) to reach their desired target group. Beyond ad targeting, advertisers use data for analytics, user profiling, modeling, website customization, and other applications.

Agencies and agency trading desks

Agencies and agency trading desks (ATDs) use data for media planning and ad targeting on behalf of their clients. They tend to use both the client's first-party as well as purchase third-party data from external vendors. Some agencies also engage in collecting data themselves – from ad campaigns they process and other sources.

Publishers

Publishers, with their web properties and mobile apps, are a major source of digital advertising data. User behavior on these properties can be tracked – either by publishers or third parties. Publishers can implement and manage data collection technology themselves (alone, or as part of a publisher co-op), or allow an external partner (typically a data vendor) to do it on their behalf. One of the primary reasons for publishers to collect data is the extra revenue it can bring when sold to interested parties. However, publishers also often use data themselves – for targeting direct and programmatic campaigns, content customization, website optimization, or analytics.

Standalone advertising platforms

Facebook, Google, Twitter, and other standalone advertising platforms thrive on data. With hundreds of millions of active users, they have unparalleled access to high-quality interest, intent, or sociodemographic data. These platforms offer efficient and relatively easy to use one-stop digital advertising solutions on their properties. Due to data scale and quality, along with the user attention they command and other factors, standalone advertising platforms have proven wildly popular with advertisers and agencies. However, they tend to control and restrict data flow outside of the platform (sometimes causing frustration on the part of advertisers), to protect their valuable data assets. Chapter 3 explores the possibilities and limitations of standalone advertising platforms in detail.

Data vendors and exchanges

Hundreds of specialized data vendors, as well as several major data exchanges, have built a business around collecting, processing, and selling data for ad targeting and other purposes. Many are widely integrated across the ecosystem, enabling them to easily transfer data to data management platforms, demand-side platforms, ad servers, content management systems, analytics platforms, and elsewhere. As for the data itself – sources, quality, and availability vary. Thus, vendor scrutiny, pre-campaign analytics, and careful testing are key to successful data purchase. Advertisers and agencies are the primary customers, using third-party data to augment their first-party data assets and increase ROI of prospecting campaigns (i.e. reaching people they do not have any first-party data on). An overview of a few dozen data vendors and exchanges can be found in Chapter 4.

Data management platforms

Data management platform (DMP) is a fairly complex piece of software used to collect, store, classify, analyze, distribute, and manage large quantities of data from various sources including web sites, mobile apps, CRM systems, or external data partners. DMPs are often used by advertisers and publishers, but also by some agencies. Around a dozen major DMP vendors exist, offering either standalone or in-stack solutions. Chapter 5 provides an introduction to data management platforms, while Chapter 6 gives an overview of top vendors.

Demand-side platforms

Demand-side platforms (DSPs) are used by advertisers and agencies to purchase ad inventory in a programmatic way, enabling campaign planning, execution, optimization, and analysis. Since programmatic media buying happens in an auction on the level of individual impressions, it is common to apply data to inform bidding decisions. DSPs typically offer data integration across many sources, from advertiser's first-party data to a host of third-party vendors. This data can be used not only for ad targeting, but also for campaign or segment analytics. Some DSPs can be purchased alongside a DMP from the same vendor (i.e. they are in the same stack), which has advantages when it comes to data flow between the two platforms. DSPs also sometimes have preferential integrations with select DMPs, so data can be transferred in (almost) real-time with minimum losses. Popular DSPs include DoubleClick, Amazon, MediaMath, DataXu, Adform, AppNexus, TheTradeDesk, Amobee, RocketFuel, or AOL.

Retargeters

Retargeters are specialized vendors, focused on maximizing yield from first-party data. At its core, retargeting is simply reaching out again to users who have visited a website, or shown interest in a product or service. Retargeters can add another layer of sophistication to this process, taking into account users' likelihood of clicking/converting among other factors. Popular retargeters include Criteo, AdRoll, ReTargeter, or RTB House.

Ad servers

Ad servers are used by advertisers and publishers to deliver digital ads. They not only serve ads, but also

help with campaign trafficking, management, optimization, tracking, reporting, and analysis. Advertisers use
ad servers to centralize their campaign management
across different media and publishers. On the other side,
publishers use them to manage and prioritize simultane-
ous campaigns from multiple clients. Similar to DSPs, ad
servers can take advantage of data for targeting – often
delivered via a DMP, or direct data vendor integration.
Some of the well-known ad servers include DoubleClick
for Advertisers/Publishers (DFA/DFP), Sizmek, Adform,
or SAS.

Data onboarders

Data onboarders help clients bring offline customer data
(e.g. from a CRM database) into the digital ecosystem. The
process is described later in this chapter. Vendors like
LiveRamp, Neustar, or some DMPs provide this service.

Tag management vendors

Tag management is a class of software used to easily
manage multiple tags (chunks of JavaScript code, frequently used for tracking and data capture) on a website.
Google Tag Manager is very common, but other vendors such as Adobe or Tealium offer tag management
solutions.

Website analytics vendors

Website analytics vendors have been around for many years, collecting first-party data on website visitors and traffic sources. These tools help with reporting, analysis (such as customer journey), visitor segmentation, or data visualization. Web analytics solutions are often offered as part of a broader digital marketing stack. Google Analytics (and Google Analytics 360) dominate this space (due in large part to being free), but other well-known players include Adobe Analytics, Webtrends, or Piwik.

Ad Measurement vendors

Ad measurement technology is a hot segment of the digital advertising ecosystem, helping advertisers deliver impartial, clean, cross-platform media data. This not only increases ecosystem transparency (alongside viewability, fraud measurement, and brand safety tools), but is key to proper attribution and media spend optimization. Some of the major vendors include Moat (recently acquired by Oracle), DoubleVerify, or Integral Ad Science.

Industry bodies and governments

Industry bodies, including Interactive Advertising Bureau (IAB), Media Rating Council (MRC), or Trustworthy

Accountability Group (TAG), serve an important role in self-regulating data collection and usage practices to protect user privacy and ecosystem integrity. In addition, government regulation is becoming increasingly impactful. For example, General Data Protection Regulation (GDPR), together with the proposed ePrivacy directive, are about to profoundly change data practices in the EU.

Data collection and transfer methods

In order to collect and transfer data across the digital advertising ecosystem, several common methods can be employed. For website environments, whether desktop or mobile, tags and pixels are typically used to capture data and send it to all relevant parties. Data onboarding is the standard procedure for bringing data from a CRM or other offline database into the online environment. App developers often implement special SDKs (Software Development Kits) to monitor users' in-app behavior and forward this data to a DMP or a data vendor. To transfer data between two web servers, either API-based direct server-to-server integration or batch processing is commonly used. Finally, cookie syncing as an underlying technology enabling data transfer is briefly discussed at the end of this section.

Tag-based collection

Tags (pieces of JavaScript and HTML code) are a standard method of collecting and transferring website data. As a webpage loads, the tag it contains is loaded and executed ("fired"). This serves to transfer explicitly defined, structured data (such as URL, page title, etc.) to a DMP or another partner, and to enable their server to set cookies. Tags are usually managed via tag managers (such as Google Tag Manager or Adobe's Dynamic Tag Management), not only to simplify deployment but also to get control over where, under what conditions, and which tags get fired. DMPs and other platforms that use tags usually provide an interface for generating them, and offer tag customization for collecting non-standard attributes. Special mobile website tags are often available. In order to work properly, tags must contain identifiers (such as client seat/ID with the tag provider, source IDs, etc.) so that the data can be correctly ingested with no risk of data leakage.

Pixel-based collection

Pixel is essentially a simpler tag – a piece of code embedded in a web page (or, quite often, in emails), used for tracking user activity or data transfer. It is usually implemented as a tiny, invisible image (1x1, or one pixel

– hence the name), referenced through a single line of HTML code. Tracking pixels are often used by third parties to monitor user activity on a particular site or across many sites. Another common use case is capturing ad campaign data (such as impressions or clicks) by "pixeling" the creative. Beyond the typical implementation noted above, any external content on a website can serve as a tracking pixel – including banner ads or social media buttons. Requests fired by pixels go to a third-party web server, enabling it to set third-party cookies. For publishers, it is therefore extremely important to know which tracking pixels are allowed on their web sites, to protect their valuable data and user privacy.

Data onboarding

Onboarding is a common technique for bringing offline data from a structured database (e.g. data warehouse, customer relationship management system, or loyalty program database) to an online environment. Data is usually onboarded into a data management platform, and formatting must adhere to the DMP specification. The process itself is fairly straightforward – data is ingested, anonymized (removing/hashing personally identifiable information), and if possible matched with online data (via common identifiers, such as hashed email address, phone number, postcode, etc.). Most DMPs offer data onboarding services – either themselves, or via an external vendor (such as LiveRamp).

Software Development Kit (SDK)

SDKs are used to collect mobile app data, and are usually offered by the collecting party (such as DMP or data vendor) for iOS and Android. SDK has to be integrated into a mobile app and configured properly in order to track user actions and collect all the data points described in Chapter 1.

Application Programming Interface (API)

APIs, in addition to other uses, facilitate the transfer of data directly between web servers (i.e. server-to-server integration), and are a common way of ingesting data into a DMP. In essence, an API specifies how a server is to be communicated with (in the form of accepted methods with implementation instructions). For example, an API might define a method for onboarding user data into a DMP. APIs can be leveraged to transfer data in real-time (or very close to real-time), or in regular intervals.

Batch data processing

With batch processing, data is transferred at set intervals (for example every hour or once a day) between web servers (one of them is often a DMP server). Correctly formatted and named files are used for this purpose, and they must follow the receiving platform's convention in terms of required content and syntax. Batch data processing is usually implemented when real-time server-to-server integration is not possible, or when timing is not critical. Common use cases are transferring data from offline and custom databases, as well as ad server log ingestion into a DMP.

Cookies and cookie syncing

In the current advertising data ecosystem, cookies play a critical role as the most prevalent user identifier. A lot of data is tied to cookies of the collecting party, and these cookies need to be synced (or matched) with a partners' cookies in order for data to be successfully transferred.

In a nutshell, cookies are small pieces of data sent from a web server and stored as text files in a web browser. Every time the web browser makes a request to a server, this data is sent back to the server along with the request. As the request is fulfilled, the web server can update its cookie in the browser as well. Cookies in each browser are separate (i.e. users with multiple browsers used to access the same web server will have multiple cookies from the server), and can be read only by the server domain which set them.

Cookies are very useful for maintaining the state of a browser session, as the HTTP protocol used for communication between browsers and web servers is stateless by design. Without cookies, a web server would treat each browser request as a separate event. Cookie is a means of letting the server know that some requests are related – together and to a particular browser (commonly taken as a proxy for user). This enables a server to remember user preferences (such as website language or currency), login state, items added to a shopping cart, and other information. When it comes to data, cookies serve primarily as an identifier to tie all related user data together. Data itself can be stored either directly in the cookie, or remotely on a web server.

Cookie syncing (also called cookie matching) is a process of pairing cookies related to the same browser/user from one ad tech platform with those of another platform. This is necessary because, as noted above, cookies can be read only by the server domain (i.e. platform) which set them and no one else. Separate platforms (such as a DMP and DSP), each having set their own cookie, require cookie syncing to know the cookies are related to the same user and data transfer is therefore possible.

Cookie syncing process between two platforms results in a match table (stored by either or both parties), which maps cookie IDs from one platform to cookie IDs from the other platform:

PLATFORM A'S USER ID	PLATFORM A'S COOKIE ID	PLATFORM B'S COOKIE ID
ABC	123	321
DEF	456	654
GHI	789	987

FIGURE 3: MATCH TABLE EXAMPLE

This is an example of how an actual sync happens using pixels:

1) User visits a website controlled by platform A (i.e. platform A can fire tags/pixels and set cookies). Synchronization pixel containing platform A's cookie ID will fire, targeted at platform B.

2) Upon receiving the sync request, platform B reads and saves platform A's cookie ID in a match table against its own cookie ID (if none exists, platform B can set a cookie at this time to create one).

3) Platform B redirects back to platform A, passing it platform B's cookie ID.

4) Platform A reads platform B's cookie ID and stores it in the match table against its own cookie ID.

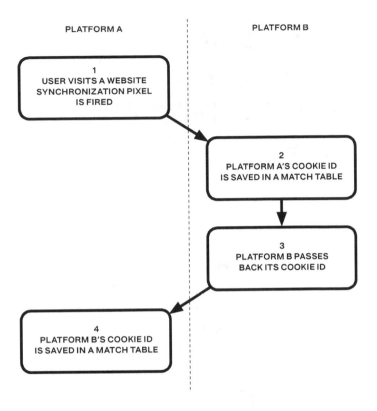

FIGURE 4: COOKIE SYNCHRONIZATION PROCESS

Now that platform A knows a user's ID used by platform B and vice versa, they can easily share data related to the same user. All that platform B needs to do is always attach its own ID whenever it transfers data to platform A (whether using tags, pixels, real-time server-to-server integration, batch processing, or even within bid requests in case of SSP/DSP communication).

Chapter 3 Standalone advertising platform data

Standalone advertising platforms such as Facebook, Google, or Amazon, are the data behemoths of today's digital ecosystem. With hundreds of millions (or even billions) of active and regular users, these platforms are able to marry massive cross-device reach with deep understanding of people's behavior, interests, and intent. Indeed, it is quality data at scale which gives them power to attract the bulk of advertisers' digital budgets, and they tend to keenly protect this valuable asset.

Standalone advertising platforms are sometimes referred to as "walled gardens" in the industry, owing to the fact that they (naturally) tend to tightly control data and place various restrictions on its flow across the platform's borders. Of course, each platform does this to a different degree and in different ways. A common limitation advertisers face is the inability to export individual-level campaign data (such as impressions and clicks) from the platform, let alone employ their own tracking. This means they cannot manage campaigns effectively across platforms – for example, there cannot be universal consistent measurement, frequency capping, or ad sequencing. In turn, cross-platform attribution and campaign optimization is very difficult – if not impossible. Advertisers also often cannot use the platform's data outside of the platform, or bring in their own audience segments for targeting (built in a DMP for example). In effect, while protecting their own control over data, standalone advertising platforms take this control away from advertisers.

Even with these limitations, which might not be important for many advertisers, standalone advertising platforms are fantastic for targeting very granular audience segments. Common targeting options include demographics, location, keywords, interests, behaviors, or intent. Advertisers can usually take advantage of advanced look-a-like modeling, based on massive data pools. Retargeting tends to be possible as well, and most platforms also enable advertisers to upload a customer list (typically in the form of email addresses) for custom targeting. In this chapter, we will look at the data options offered by Facebook, Google AdWords, Amazon, Twitter, LinkedIn, eBay, Snapchat, and Pinterest.

Facebook and Instagram

Facebook[2], the largest global social network with over 2 billion monthly active users[3], offers a treasure trove of data for targeting across Facebook, Instagram, and beyond. Advertisers can take advantage of so-called Core Audiences, as well as tailored Custom Audiences.

Core Audiences

Demographic targeting on Facebook, Instagram, and across Facebook's Audience Network can be very specific, and supported by heaps of declared data. At the basic level, campaigns can be restricted by age (very granular, range is adjustable by single years), gender, and language. Other options include education (education level, fields of study, schools/universities), household composition, life events (such as anniversary, birthday, new job, recent move, being away from family, or even being a friend of newly engaged people), parental status (new parents, parents with teenagers, etc.), political views (US only; conservative/moderate/liberal) relationship status (married, single, complicated, etc.) or work (employer, industry, job title).

Location targeting is enabled on a country, state, province/region, city, zip/postal code, and specific location ("pin") level. Businesses that want to reach people near their physical locations can take advantage of business location targeting. Although the default option is targeting everyone in a chosen location, other possibilities include people who live there, who got there recently, or who are traveling there.

Connections targeting is based on how an audience is connected to a business – either to its Facebook page, app(s), or events. For Facebook pages and apps, options include people or friends of people who have liked or used it (or not yet). For events, people who have (or not yet) responded to an event.

Interest targeting uses data such as Facebook user's listed interests, activities, pages they like, groups they belong to, education, or job title. Interests are grouped into categories, such as business and industry, entertainment, fitness and wellness, technology, or hobbies and activities. These are further split into sub-categories – for example, sports and outdoors includes things like fishing, surfing, mountain biking, marathons, or golf, while business and industry is divided into areas such as advertising, healthcare, small business, or science.

Behavior targeting covers mainly purchase behavior or intent, but also device usage and other activities. Top-level categories include for instance automotive, B2B, media, purchase behavior, or residential profiles. Naturally, more granular targeting is possible. The automotive category, for example, includes a sub-category of in-market vehicle shoppers, who may be targeted by vehicle make they intend to buy. Interesting audiences include expats, company executives, engaged shoppers, or likely investors. Audiences for behavior targeting are often supplied by third-party vendors such as Oracle or Acxiom.

Custom Audiences

Custom Audiences enable the use of a client's first-party data for targeting on Facebook. First-party data can take the form of a user list (of email addresses, phone numbers, etc.), website visitors, or app users. Unlike Twitter for example, cookie IDs cannot be matched to create a custom audience.

First of all, a custom audience can be created by uploading and matching a list containing user identifiers such as email address, phone number, mobile advertiser ID (Apple's IDFA or Android's advertising ID), first name and surname, zip/postcode, date of birth, gender, Facebook app user ID, or Facebook page user ID. The more identifiers are supplied, the higher match rate with Facebook users can be expected.

Another option is to create a custom audience from website visitors using Facebook's pixel (a piece of code implemented on client's website). In addition to simply tracking all visitors across the website, special events can be set up (such as purchase, lead, search, adding to cart, or completing a registration) to create more actionable audiences. Facebook SDK can be used to track app users in a similar fashion.

To increase reach, look-a-like modeling helps find users similar to a custom audience from a client's list. In addition, look-a-like audiences can be built from Facebook page fans and website visitors collected via Facebook pixel.

Google AdWords

Google AdWords[4] is a major gateway to Google's advertising ecosystem (alongside DoubleClick for example), letting clients run a variety of campaign types on Google Search Network and Google Display Network. AdWords offers a wide range of targeting options, dependent both on campaign type (e.g. search, video, display or shopping) and the network used for ad delivery. Below is a quick overview to give an idea of what is possible – however, with the right tools, budget, and experience, very complex, dynamic, and automated targeting can be achieved. Beyond targeting, Google AdWords can provide other valuable data. For example, AdWords can be connected to client's Google Analytics for attribution, measurement, testing, and analytical purposes.

Google Search Network

On Google Search Network (a group of search-related websites operated by Google, including search results, Google Maps, or search partners), ads can be targeted by keywords, location, language, demographics, devices, or retargeting audiences.

Keyword targeting lets advertisers pick words or phrases their customers are likely to search for, and display their ads alongside search results to ensure relevance and campaign performance. Keywords can be matched in different ways, including broad match, phrase match, exact match, negative match, or match with modifier. There are many specialized books on AdWords/PPC (pay-per click) advertising, which go in depth on how to run keyword-based campaigns on Google. What needs to be noted though, is the sheer power of search data – manifested in the growth and value of Google itself. In essence, keywords used while searching are a very strong signal of intent or interest – this is some of the most valuable data in digital advertising today. Coupled with AdWords platform, which enables absolutely granular and custom auction-based targeting, there are not many performance channels that can compete in efficiency.

In addition to keywords, ads can be targeted by location, language, and demographics. Ad campaign can be targeted at a specific geographic location, such as country, region, or city. Users' language for targeting purposes is determined by several factors, including Google domain used, search terms, IP address, or language preferences. As for demographics, options include age (in 5-year brackets), gender, and household income (in deciles for the top households). Selected devices can be targeted as well, such as computers, tablets, or mobile phones.

Dynamic search ads, an automated search advertis-ing solution, use content of an advertiser's website (i.e. page titles or frequently used phrases) to target ads to user searches and dynamically create headlines and landing pages.

Google Search Network also supports retargeting of clients' website visitors via RLSA (Remarketing Lists for Search Ads). A retargeting audience can be created by placing Google's tag on one or multiple website pages – minimum audience size is 1,000 users. This audience (or multiple audiences/combinations) can be used for search campaign targeting, and letting advertisers create custom ads/bidding strategies for retargeted users.

Finally, a fairly recent targeting option for search is Customer Match – audience targeting based on an email address list uploaded to Google and matched against Google's database. Advertisers are able to target matched users when they are signed in and searching on Google.

Google Display Network

Google Display Network is a collection of more than 2 million websites, videos, and apps. Targeting options include location, language, demographics, device, keywords, topics, placements, audiences, and automated tools.

Similar to Google Search Network, the Display Network lets advertisers target by location, language, demographics (also including parental status), or devices.

Audience targeting enables not only retargeting (static or dynamic), but also prospecting – by reaching out to unknown people based on their interests or purchase intent. Affinity-based audiences, split into a large number of categories and subcategories, are groups of people sharing a long-term interest (e.g. shutterbugs, cooking enthusiasts, avid investors, or fashionistas). Custom affinity audiences can be created as well, based on words, phrases, or URLs an audience might be interested in. In-market audiences comprise people actively researching products (such as office supplies, sports tickets, residential properties for sale, sporting goods, or car rental).

Keyword targeting comes in two flavors – content keywords and audience keywords. Content keywords serve to target relevant websites, apps, and videos on the Display Network (i.e. keywords are matched to content). Audience keywords let advertisers target relevant audiences who browse content about those keywords (here, keywords are matched to audience interests).

Topic targeting allows ads to be displayed on pages related to a chosen topic. Web page topics/central themes are determined through analysis of text, language, link, and page structure. Topics cover a wide range of areas, including for example mountain bikes, poetry, fishing, smart phones, or investment banking.

Placement targeting simply restricts an ad campaign to chosen websites, YouTube channels, YouTube videos, apps, or app categories.

Automated targeting works as audience extension, reaching people outside the set targeting while maintaining similar cost per person. Options include conservative targeting (narrow extension) and aggressive targeting (broad extension, also called "Display Campaign Optimizer"). Automated targeting can be also used for retargeting.

Google recently introduced another automated targeting solution, called smart display campaigns. This automates and optimizes not only targeting (combining contextual, audience-based, or retargeting), but also bidding and ad creation.

YouTube and video partners on the Display Network

Video ads can use targeting as well, not only on YouTube but also when played by Google's video partners. Although formally a part of Google Display Network, video ads deserve a separate section.

Standard targeting options include language, location, demographics (age, gender, parental status, household income), and devices. Audience targeting is available, with audiences based on affinity, in-market behavior, or belonging to a retargeting pool. A special video retargeting feature is available for YouTube, where retargeting audiences are created based on interactions with videos or YouTube channel. Content targeting can be either based around keywords, topics, or specific placements (such as selected YouTube channels or videos). Customer match is also available for YouTube, with an option to extend reach with a similar (look-a-like) audience.

Google Shopping

Google Shopping (primarily available on the Search Network, but also on YouTube), tackles targeting from a different angle to suit retailers with large product catalogues. Search queries related to products from an advertiser's Merchant Center product feed are automatically targeted, with no need (or option) to set up keyword targeting. Only negative keywords (keywords excluded from a campaign) are permitted, to prevent ads from appearing next to undesirable search results. Google Shopping ads can be also targeted for example by location, country of sale, device, or Google ad network. Customer Match can be used with Google Shopping as well.

Amazon

Amazon[5] is waking up to challenge Facebook and Google in the digital advertising space, taking advantage of the opportunity offered by its unparalleled access to customer data. It has been widely reported that Amazon is the most popular destination to begin a product search[6] – and when it comes to completing purchases, it plays in a different league to everyone else with over 43 % US online market share[7]. In addition to purchase data from its sites, Amazon has access to other sources as well – including media consumption data via Amazon Prime Video/Music and Kindle, voice search data through Alexa, or offline data from physical stores (including Whole Foods). Amazon has started scaling up its advertising business recently, switching largely to self-service and hiring sales staff at a very fast rate[8]. With a unique visibility of the entire purchase funnel, Amazon is positioned to become the currency when it comes to campaign attribution and optimization – particularly for brands relying heavily on external sales channels. As one of the few platforms out there, Amazon has an extensive, deterministic (login based) cross-device ID graph. This not only helps stitch data across devices, but enables precise measurement and attribution. Amazon data can be activated through a proprietary DSP, called Amazon Advertising Platform (AAP)[9], or via Amazon Marketing Services (AMS)[10].

Amazon Advertising Platform lets clients access a wide selection of inventory across Amazon owned and operated sites and apps (such as Amazon.com or IMDb.com), as well as leading publishers' sites, apps, and exchanges[11]. Several data categories are currently available for audience targeting on AAP, including lifestyle, in-market, contextual, look-a-like, retargeting, demographics, and geolocation. Lifestyle segments (together with in-market) are behavioral, based on historical search, browsing, and purchase history up to the past year. For example, the "Video Gamers" segment comprises customers who have browsed or purchased products from the Video Game product category over the past 12 months. In-market segments are built from customers who have recently browsed for a product within a specific category. Contextual targeting is based on the detail page a consumer is actively viewing – targeted ads simply appear alongside selected products or categories. Look-a-like segments can be modeled from website audiences collected using Amazon pixel, customer match audiences (more detail on this follows), or from Amazon's data. Retargeting (just like Google, Amazon calls it "remarketing") is available as well, either based on standard client's first-party data (collected via website pixel/customer match), or on Amazon's data – as product listing retargeting. Finally, demographic and geo targeting includes age, gender, location, household income level, or the number of children in a household[12].

Amazon Marketing Services is a pay-per-click platform suitable for performance campaigns, available to Amazon vendors and Kindle Direct Publishing (KDP) authors. Ads are displayed in the search results, alongside product listings, or even on enabled Kindle e-readers. Targeting can be based on selected keywords, products, or interests (taking users' category interests as a proxy)[13].

Similar to other digital advertising platforms, Amazon offers a self-serve audience match tool called Advertiser Audiences. This enables advertisers to create targeting segments from their own customer lists for use on Amazon. A list of at least 20,000 email addresses, either hashed or unhashed (to be hashed by the browser in the upload process), is required. Customers who are matched successfully fall into an Advertiser Audience, which can be activated directly for targeting (or exclusion), or used for look-a-like modeling[14].

Twitter

Twitter[15], the bite-size broadcasting social network, has around 330 million monthly active users[16]. It offers both proprietary and third-party data, as well as targeting based on first-party data called "Tailored Audiences."

Proprietary and third-party data

Twitter offers a number of basic targeting options based on proprietary or third-party data. These include demographics and technical data, keywords, interests, followers, events, TV preferences, and behaviors. Some of the targeting options can be combined into specific custom audiences, but not all combinations are possible. Also, targeting options differ by region. The following overview gives a taste of what is possible without using clients' first-party data.

First of all, Twitter campaigns can be targeted by demographics and technical data, including gender (mostly inferred from names/follow graphs), age (not available to all advertisers), language, device, platform, location (e.g. country, state, region, metro area, postal/zip code), or carrier.

Second, keywords can be used for targeting. Here, keywords in users' search queries, recent tweets, or tweets they recently engaged with are considered. Keyword matching options are available, including broad (default), phrase, negative, or negative phrase match. Tweets in which keywords appear with a negative sentiment can be filtered out.

Third, Twitter users can be targeted based on their interests. Interest categories include for example books and literature, careers, life stages, personal finances, or business. Categories are broken down into more granular subcategories. To illustrate, "business" category is further divided into areas like marketing, entrepreneurship, small business, or business software. Similarly, "personal finances" include stocks, insurance, credit/loans, banking, retirement planning, etc.

Fourth, clients have an option to select "follower" targeting. Ads are displayed to people who have similar interests to followers of selected usernames. This targeting can be optionally extended by also including clients' own followers, or users who are similar to clients' own followers.

Fifth, users can be targeted based on the events they are interested in. Events include sports, entertainment, movie releases, conferences, holidays, or political events.

Sixth, thanks to TV targeting, campaigns can be aimed at people who engage with selected TV shows, genres, or networks. When targeting by selected TV show (or set of shows), users can be reached either continuously throughout the campaign, or only around new show airings.

Finally, users can be targeted based on their behaviors – they could be for example classified as corporate execs, Renault owners, foodies, wives, horse racing fans, or toys buyers. Data for behavioral targeting is often provided by third-party vendors, such as Datalogix (Oracle) or Acxiom.

Tailored Audiences

Tailored Audiences let clients use their own first-party data for targeting on Twitter, for either retargeting or prospecting campaigns. Tailored Audiences can be also used to activate clients' preferred third-party data (combined or not with first-party data) from an external vendor, otherwise unavailable directly on Twitter. Tailored Audiences come in three main types – either created from lists, mobile apps, or web.

Tailored Audiences from lists are created by uploading email addresses, mobile phone numbers, Twitter IDs (either user IDs or usernames), or mobile advertising IDs (iOS advertising IDs, Google advertising IDs, or Android

IDs). The list is matched with Twitter users, and those who are successfully matched can be targeted on Twitter. A minimum of 500 users must be matched to create an audience from a list, so the original list needs to be significantly longer. In addition to being able to upload lists from within Twitter Ads UI, there are partners who can manage audiences via API – including Acxiom, Datalogix, LiveRamp, MailChimp, and others.

Mobile Apps-based Tailored Audiences are built from users of a mobile app, collected through conversion tracking. Audience segments are created for specific conversion events in the app, such as install or sign up. These segments can then be used for retargeting, exclusion from campaigns, or other targeting tactics on Twitter.

The last, and a very interesting option is Tailored Audiences from web. These audiences can be composed of visitors to a website who complete a given action (such as site visit, purchase, download, or sign up), and are great for retargeting campaigns on Twitter. Setting this up is very straightforward, and can be easily accomplished using Twitter's website tag.

However, Tailored Audiences from web are not limited to website retargeting – in fact, audiences can be built from any pool of cookie IDs pushed to Twitter by one of their partners (such as Lotame, MediaMath, BlueKai, and others). This can be incredibly powerful, as it allows advertisers to target any audience from a DMP or other partner platform on Twitter – including audiences from their first-party data, second-party data, third-party data, or a combination of the three. Once the cookie IDs are pushed to Twitter, a matching process (similar to the one in list-based audiences) determines actual reach.

A potentially valuable option for tailored audiences is look-a-like modeling, whereby these audiences can be extended by similar users based on interests, location, demographics, or engagement patterns. Look-a-like only targeting (i.e. excluding the seed audience) is possible as well, which can be useful for prospecting campaigns.

LinkedIn

As the largest professional network with over 500 million members[17], LinkedIn[18] offers a wealth of unique, high-quality data largely declared by users themselves. This data can be useful for business-to-business, work-related, or general ad targeting on LinkedIn and beyond (via the LinkedIn Audience Network). LinkedIn offers both a broad selection of targetable demographic characteristics, first-party contact list targeting (called "Matched Audiences"), as well as website retargeting.

Demographic targeting options include location, company name, company industry, company size, company connections (first-degree connections of employees at selected companies), followers (of your own company page), job title, job function, job seniority, schools, fields of study, degrees, skills, groups, gender, age, and years of experience[19].

LinkedIn Matched Audiences is similar to Facebook's Custom Audiences or Google's Customer Match. Advertisers can upload either a list of companies (i.e. an account list composed of company names and website URLs) or contacts (an individual email list) they would like to target. LinkedIn will then try and match contacts on the list with their users, and create a targetable audience with minimum size of 300 matched users. For more advanced clients, LinkedIn can directly integrate with contact management platforms such as Marketo, Eloqua, LiveRamp, or Axciom, so manual list uploading is not necessary. Advertisers can also retarget website visitors on LinkedIn by placing a tag, and have the option to augment this with demographic data available on the platform.

eBay

With 168 million active buyers worldwide[20], eBay[21] has fantastic access to large-scale data on purchase intent, interests, and shopping behavior. Data can be used both on eBay websites, as well as across a network of partner sites and apps called eBay Audience Platform. To make life easier for advertisers, eBay categorizes data offerings into three buckets – "Building Blocks", "Personas" and more advanced "Audience Matching & Modeling[22]".

eBay Building Blocks are made up of demographic (age, gender, net worth, employment), geographic, household (income, marital status, home ownership, pet ownership, parental status), and technographic (carrier, laptop/tablet/smartphone ownership, device preferences) data, alongside buying, selling and behavior-based category intent and interest segments. For example, buyer categories include top buyers, big spenders, cost-conscious shoppers, or eBay loyalists. Interest and purchase intent segments comprise audiences such as Cameras & Photo, Consumer Electronics, Sports Memorabilia, or Art. Seasonal segments, such as Fathers' Day shoppers or Football Fanatics interested in Super Bowl are available as well.

Personas, or multifaceted audiences built from eBay Building Blocks, can be either ready-made (i.e. "Classics") or custom ("Originals"). Examples of classic segments include Yogis, New & Expecting Moms, Pop Culture Connoisseurs, Philanthropists, DIYers, or Shutterbugs. Small Business owners, whether eBay sellers or buyers, are also available for targeting. eBay offers the option of building custom, original segments for their advertising clients.

eBay, like other standalone advertising platforms, enables clients to upload CRM lists to be matched with eBay users for ad targeting. Shop-alike modeling (a variant of look-a-like modeling based on shopping data) is available.

Snapchat

Snapchat[23], a popular platform with young membership base, offers several ad targeting options. Advertisers can choose demographic and device targeting, predefined interest-based audiences, and custom solutions.

Demographic targeting options include age (in brackets for younger audiences, up to 35+), gender, language, and in some markets also household income or parental status. Targetable devices are split by operating systems, brands, models, and carriers.

Snapchat also offers over 300 predefined audiences based around interests and behaviors, built from Snapchat and third-party data. Audience segments include for example "Automotive Enthusiasts", "Home Decoristas", or "Film & TV Fans" (further split into genres).

Advertisers can also take advantage of custom audiences. Snap Audience Match works like similar services on other advertising platforms – a list of user emails or mobile advertising IDs is uploaded to create an audience.

This audience can be further extended using built-in look-a-like modeling capability.

Pinterest

Pinterest[24], a visual social network (or, as the CEO Ben Silbermann likes to say, a "catalogue of ideas[25]"), has over 200 million members around the world. It also offers targeting based on user data, which reveals their interests, aspirations, and often purchase intent. Targeting options include gender, device, language, location, keywords, interests, and custom audiences.

Keyword targeting enables advertisers to reach users when they search on Pinterest. Keyword match types (broad, exact, or phrase), as well as negative keywords are available.

Pinterest offers more than 6,000 interest segments, grouped into broader categories such as Design, Fashion, or Products. However, advertisers can drill down to very specific interests, such as "iPhone" or "Package Tours".

Perhaps the most interesting targeting option is Pinterest Audiences[26]. These are custom segments built from advertiser's website visitors (collected via Pinterest Tag), uploaded customer lists (emails or mobile ad IDs), people who engaged with Pins from the advertiser's website, or look-a-like (called "actalike") audiences.

Chapter 4
Data vendors and exchanges

This chapter takes a detailed look at some of the best-known data providers and exchanges – from massive marketplaces like Oracle Data Cloud and Lotame Data Exchange (LDX) to more specialized vendors. It would be impossible to offer a profile of every data vendor, and impractical to include even the top one hundred. This chapter therefore focuses on a few dozen selected players, widely integrated across the ecosystem.

The aim is to give a taste of which categories of data can be purchased for targeting and other purposes, and provide a starting point for further research. It is important to note that the selection of available data vendors (and data they sell) is very much market specific. Although many vendors operate globally, they might not have a significant presence in some markets. On the other hand, hundreds of regional publishers, data co-ops and smaller vendors operate locally – often with better data offerings than the big players. It is critical that a thorough data testing takes place when onboarding a new vendor, as data quality varies greatly.

There are many good reasons why digital advertisers, agencies, and even publishers might purchase data from third parties. Perhaps the most common use case is basic ad targeting to reach a desired audience. More advanced clients combine third-party data with their own for user profiling and other analytics. Facilitated by many DMPs, third-party data can be handily used for look-a-like modeling/audience extension. Other applications include for example benchmarking, content/ad personalization, or data verification.

Third-party data vendors sell a wide variety of data, including demographics, interest, intent, lifestyle, B2B, location, or identity. When selecting a vendor, clients should always enquire about data sources and creation methods. Typically, declared data from a reputable source tends to be the most accurate.

Without further ado, individual vendor and data exchange profiles follow in alphabetical order.

33across

33across[27] is a New York based publisher monetization and traffic platform with global reach. The company collects behavioral data from over 1 million websites, covering 1.4 billion users. Data signals include content consumption, search keywords, copy and paste sharing, or social behaviors. 33across offers audience segments such as auto, fashion, travel, finance, or beauty, and is integrated with many DMPs, DSPs, and other platforms.

Acxiom

Acxiom[28] is a leading global provider of consumer and household data, based in the United States. With a long history and access to a wide range of both offline and online data sources, Acxiom is a vendor with scale, as well as unique matching and identity resolution capabilities (marketed as "AbiliTec"). To effectively manage the wealth of data on offer, clients can use Acxiom Audience Cloud – a self-serve tool for building custom segments. Apart from standard data categories, special data packages built around events (such as sports or Valentine's Day) are available. The so-called "Personicx" multi-dimensional segmentation solution provides clusters of similar users, complete with behavioral and demographic profiles. There are specific clusters which might be suitable for different client needs, including lifestyle, financial, or Hispanic market versions. Acxiom is widely integrated within the digital ecosystem, with more than 400 partners.

Affinity Answers

Affinity Answers[29], a US company headquartered in Austin, specializes in monitoring and analyzing brand-related engagement activity across social media including Facebook, Twitter, and Instagram. The company monitors over 400 million consumers' active engagement behavior (such as comments or retweets) towards more than 60,000 brands. There are over 2,000 standard segments available organized into categories like "Beauty Products Influencers", "Retail", or "Automotive Makes & Models". Custom segments can be defined as well, and data is also available for audience extension.

ALC

ALC[30], a US company, prides itself on data which is not modeled or inferred, but aggregated from original sources. User profiles are anchored to a physical location (i.e. postal address), and can be used for both offline and online targeting. "ALC B2B" offers over 230 segments (sliced by industry, revenue, title, function, etc.), enabling clients to reach business decision makers. "ALC MD+" is a product covering healthcare professionals, with over 200 segments. "ALC Auto+" enables targeting within the automotive market, with granular data (such as make, model, class, or fuel type) based on ownership records and other verified proprietary sources. The "Newborn Network" includes new and expecting parents, while "Political Precision" offers voter data in over 500 segments. Finally, "Wealth Window" gives access to the top 1 % of consumers. ALC data is available through data exchanges or via direct integrations with major ecosystem platforms.

Alliant

Alliant[31] is a US company, offering "Alliant Online Audiences" for targeting across major DMPs, DSPs, and data exchanges. Audience segments cover 115 million US households, and are largely based on transactional data aggregated from D2C brands. Segment categories include automotive, demographic, purchase, or buying propensity. Consumer clusters/composites are available as well, such as "Moms who shop like crazy".

Analytics IQ

Analytics IQ[32] is a marketing analytics company, specializing in data science and cognitive psychology. With a pool of data aggregated from public and proprietary sources, the company builds models to predict attributes across a number of consumer behaviors and characteristics. For example, the "WealthIQ" data product contains attributes related to individual net worth – ranging from "Very High" to "Not at all High". AnalyticsIQ provides demographic, financial, behavioral, health, automotive, or psychological data.

Bombora

Bombora[33] is a well-known B2B data provider, covering over 400 million professionals across all industries. Bombora operates a data cooperative across more than 3,500 sites, with many B2B data contributors – ranging from large publishers to specialized niche destinations. Main data types include B2B Intent (based on content consumption of professionals doing product research prior to purchase) and B2B demographics (including attributes such as company size, revenue, or industry).

CACI

CACI[34] is a UK provider of data and analytics services, with a long history in data collection, management, and segmentation. The company prides itself on having the most comprehensive consumer database in the UK, with data sourced from over 75 providers (research surveys, government data, open data, etc.). As part of its "Online Audiences" product, CACI offers its well-known segmentation solutions for use in digital environments. These include Acorn (consumer classification at postcode level, based on demographic data, social factors, population, and consumer behavior), Fresco (financial services segmentation based on a combination of CACI's proprietary data and GfK Financial Research Survey, and Ocean (UK population database with 450+ lifestyle and demographic variables).

Cardlytics

Cardlytics[35] runs loyalty and rewards programs for over 1,500 banks and financial institutions in the US and UK, giving the company access to purchase data at scale. Cardlytics has visibility of credit, debit, bill pay and ACH (Automated Clearing House) transactions of tens of millions of individuals, with data gathered and segmented in a privacy-compliant manner. Audiences are segmented by merchant, spend, frequency, category, and other criteria. Standard categories include retail, travel, entertainment, services, etc., while seasonal categories such as Halloween or Valentine's day are available as well. Cardlytics can build on-demand custom segments too.

comScore TV Viewing

Following a merger with Rentrak, comScore[36] is now a leading TV and cross-platform media measurement

DATA IN DIGITAL ADVERTISING

company based in the US. It offers over 300 "TV Essentials" segments for targeting, based on data from over 20 million US households. These segments are based on genre (e.g. Reality, Movies, News, Kids, Cooking, Travel, etc.), daypart (such as weekday/weekend Prime, Daytime, Overnight, Early or Late Fringe) or Network (e.g. CBS, ESPN, CNN, Cinemax, etc.). This data might be valuable to clients running parallel TV and digital campaigns, enabling them to reach the same audience across channels.

Connexity

Connexity[37] (previously called Shopzilla), is a US company based in Los Angeles operating in the US, the UK, France, Germany, Italy, Australia, and New Zealand. The company operates a network of online retail marketplaces, giving it access to high quality purchase intent data. The "In-Market Shoppers" segments are built on data from over 175 million product listings, and broken down into 1,400 categories and 7,500 brands. Connexity also offers seasonal segments (holidays, back to school, Super Bowl, etc.), lifestyle and life stage segments, as well as demographic targeting (survey-based declared data). In addition to standard segments, Connexity also offers custom targeting and look-a-like modeling.

Cross Pixel

Cross Pixel[38] collects data on over 240 million users across e-commerce, transactional, and information websites. Audience segments (including 500+ in-market shopping segments, 450+ audience profiles, and 100+ B2B segments) can be accessed and combined using the "Audience Calculator" tool. Cross Pixel has integrations with a number of programmatic platforms (including MediaMath, Turn, or Oracle BlueKai) and covers several markets (such as UK, France, Spain, or Mexico).

Cuebiq

Cuebiq[39] is a location intelligence company, specializing in real-world location data provision and analysis. Data is collected via SDK, and includes Wi-Fi, GPS, and beacon location signals. Taking into account visit frequency and dwell time, Cuebiq distills this data into 190+ Geo-Behavioral audiences (e.g. frequent moviegoers), over 900 brand-based audiences (such as McDonald's frequent diners), and 80+ internet of things-based audiences. Data is also available for offline attribution analysis and other analytics applications.

Experian

Experian[40] is a consumer credit reporting agency operating in 37 countries, with global headquarters in Dublin. It collects data on over 1 billion individuals, with very deep knowledge of over 230 million consumers in the US and 50 million in the UK. As part of its marketing services, Experian offers a wealth of consumer, household, and business data widely available throughout the digital ecosystem.

Experian is known for its Mosaic lifestyle segmentation of households – in the US, for example, Mosaic divides the household population into 19 groups (such as "Families in Motion" or "Power Elite") and more granular sub-groups. With its credit reporting background, Experian is uniquely positioned to provide financial data. In the UK, for example, the company offers so-called "Financial Strategy Segments". On the household level, the population is split into segments such as "Bright Futures" or "Traditional Thrift". Experian also offers an interesting segmentation based on communication channel and engagement preferences, called "TrueTouch". Demographic data can be used as well, with many attributes – from the expected (such as age, gender, education, or presence of children) to more exclusive (current home value or length of residence). In general, data availability varies by region, and some of the products are market specific.

Eyeota

Eyeota[41] is a global data aggregator and vendor, with data sourced from over 30,000 publishers and data suppliers (including Experian, Bombora, Semasio, or CACI). Clients get access to more than 3.5 billion profiles across Europe, APAC and Americas, categorized into 5,800+ audience segments (including sociodemography, interests, purchase intent or B2B). Eyeota is widely integrated with top ad buying platforms and other ecosystem players.

Financial Audiences

Financial Audiences[42] provides data segments focused on finance and investing, built from data aggregated across a specialized publisher network. Data signals are a combination of content consumption, behaviors (such as comments, shares, etc.) along with registrations analysis. Segment groups include personal finance (with categories such as Insurance, banking, or retirement, further split into more granular sub-categories), business finance (insurance, lending, banking), individual investing (general investors or active traders by market), and professional investing. Demographic data as well as custom audiences are available too.

IRI

IRI[43], a global market research company based in the US, caters mostly to CPG companies with PoS (Point-of-Sale), panel, and loyalty card data and related services. IRI data is available in the digital ecosystem via selected providers, and clients can pick from several products. IRI ProScores Audiences is predictive purchase data derived from IRI Consumer Network household panel, helping to identify top spending shoppers across product categories, subcategories, and brands. IRI Verified Audiences uses purchase data from over 350 million loyalty cards. And finally, IRI Custom Audiences take advantage of IRI Audience Builder – here, clients can combine ProScores and Verified Audiences, along with other data sources to create custom audiences.

Kantar Shopcom

Kantar, a division of WPP, is a leading global provider of data, analytics, and consulting services. Kantar Shopcom[44] is a solution by Kantar Worldpanel, and offers a multi-channel customer level database (called "Shopcom Data Platform") built from a blend of CPG, retail, and trade shopper data. This data, covering 90 % of the US households, is gathered from 450+ retailers across 680 categories. Audiences can be built using Shopcom Purchase Behavior Data, as well as Shopcom Purchase Propensity Scores.

KBM Data Services

The iBehavior database[45], owned by KBM Data Services, contains consumer and business transaction data from over 2,800 contributing merchants. Audiences are divided into consumer and B2B groups – consumer segments span demographics, purchase data, media consumption, retail, and seasonal audiences, while B2B segments include firmographics or business purchase categories. Data is available in multiple countries, such as the US, the UK, Canada, France, or Brazil.

Lotame Data Exchange

Lotame Data Exchange (LDX)[46], one of the largest data marketplaces, offers consolidated audience segments built with data from over 150 different providers. LDX data covers over 4 billion cookies and mobile device IDs, ensuring broad campaign reach.

Categorization into segments is accomplished by human analysts rather than algorithms, combining layers of user characteristics (such as age, interests, and other factors) to arrive at attractive and granular segments. Over 4,000 pre-packaged and custom segments are currently available, split into categories including demographics, interest, intent, B2B, location, or smart TV audiences. These are further divided into several levels of sub-categories. For example, interest segments comprise sub-categories such as entertainment, finance, travel, or automobiles. Automobiles are then broken down by type, brands, or models.

LDX strives to match customer needs, while constantly improving data quality. Segments on the exchange undergo regular audits, where they are re-evaluated, edited, added, or removed. Through Lotame's partnership with Are You a Human, identified bots have been scrubbed from all of the profiles. Lotame also validates demographic data against Nielsen to ensure maximum quality. LDX is well integrated across the ecosystem, available across many DSPs and other platforms clients use to execute ad campaigns.

Mastercard Audiences

Mastercard[47] offers audience segments built from anonymized data capturing brick & mortar and online transactions, made with more than 2.2 billion payment cards. Clients can for example target "Top Tier Spenders" – individuals who are likely to spend two or more times the average person – split by vertical (e.g. retail, travel, or entertainment) and category (such as luxury retailer, online shopper, or sporting goods). In addition to standard segments, "Top Tier Spenders" are also segmented for seasonal events such as holidays or summer travel. From a slightly different perspective, "Frequent Transactors" – individuals who are likely to shop two or more times as often as the average person – can also be targeted by category.

Merkle

Merkle[48] is a global performance marketing agency operating across 28 offices around the world, with its own data sourcing and provision. It maintains its DataSource customer marketing database, where data is verified within proprietary Data Optimization Lab to ensure quality. Data categories, split into 500+ segments, include demographics (age, education, marital status, etc.), wealth, property, lifestyle (self-reported data including interests such as fitness, reading, or cooking), auto (make, model, and style of vehicle), and CAMEO (socio-economic indicators).

Mobilewalla

With headquarters in the US, Mobilewalla[49] offers mobile audience data in 20 countries across North America, Europe, and Asia. The in-app audiences are based on device ID, and can be used for targeting both on iOS and Android. Data is sourced from public data sources as well as extracted from impressions and interactions generated while running mobile campaigns. Mobilewalla monitors mobile behavior of hundreds of millions of users, giving its data scale and depth for both broad and highly targeted campaigns. There are hundreds of ready-made audience segments to pick from, covering everything from sports, retail, real estate, to business or health. In addition, Mobilewalla offers its clients custom segment creation for more specific targeting needs.

Navegg

Navegg[50] is a Brazil based data provider with focus on Latin America. Audience segments are built from browsing behavior data collected across top publishers, price comparison, and e-commerce platforms across Latin America. Navegg offers more than 1,400 segments, including demographics (age, social class, gender, etc.), purchase intent (such as smartphone, real estate, or museum tickets), interests (e.g. sports, entertainment), personality & lifestyle (cluster segmentation called "Everyone"), B2B, brand affinity (in vehicles, electronics, fashion, or home appliances categories), or pre-built look-a-like segments (called "Everybuyer").

Neustar AdAdvisor

Neustar[51], in addition to a DMP, offers data under the "AdAdvisor Audiences" product umbrella. Audience segments are built from both probabilistic and deterministic data, gathered across more than 200 data providers. Audience groups include automotive, demographics, personal finance, shopping, technology & computing, and many others. At a more granular level, audience groups are split into more specific sub-categories and further into audience segments – for instance automotive includes auto insurance providers (e.g. Geico), vehicle type/make (such as Ford), number of vehicles in the household, or financing.

Nielsen DMP Data

Nielsen[52,] a global market research, data, and measurement company, offers not only a DMP, but also its own Data-as-a-Service (DaaS) solution, which provides access to Nielsen audience data and third-party partner data across more than 60,000 segments. Nielsen's buyer-based audiences cover credit card spending, store visits, basket size, and product purchases at SKU-level. Data for the buyer-based audiences is collected from many sources including Nielsen Buyer Insights (85% of all credit card purchases in the US and UK), Nielsen Catalina

Solutions (140 million SKU-level FMCG purchases across the US), Nielsen Homescan Shopper Panel (one of the biggest shopping panels in the world), and J.D. Power (a large percentage of total car sales in the US).

Clients can also customize their audience data strategy around highly granular consumer attributes including demographics, psychographics, mobile, online, TV (linear and connected), and audio (terrestrial and streaming) behavior. TV data is gathered via Nielsen's industry-leading deterministic TV panel, Nielsen Gracenote's Smart TV (data is collected in real time using patented Video Automatic Content Recognition technology), and via partnerships with OTT-TV and set-top-box providers. Audio data is gathered from Nielsen's Portable People Meter (PPM) technology. This device captures tune-in behavior of more than 70,000 terrestrial listeners in the top 48 radio metros in the U.S., collecting and reporting station-identifying data.

Digital behavior and demographic data is gathered from Nielsen's proprietary and highly curated mix of offline and online data. It is sourced from more than 200 anonymous data providers, carefully audited against Nielsen's data quality and recency standards before being added to the Nielsen Marketing Cloud ecosystem. They include credit card companies, socio-demographic compilers, consumer panels, shopping engines, retail transaction aggregators, business directories, or e-commerce and retail data co-ops.

Nielsen mobile data covers over 10 billion devices worldwide and is a combination of proprietary and partner data.

Clients also have access to a wide spectrum of audience data from the Nielsen Marketing Cloud partner network, including fast-moving consumer goods (FMCG), travel, telecom, retail, auto, finance, and B2B audiences.

OneAudience

OneAudience[53] is a mobile data intelligence provider, offering over 150 audience segments across more than 400 million devices. App usage and mobile device data is gathered through a network of app developers and publishers via integrated OneAudience SDK. Audience segment categories include in-market (for example auto, travel, insurance), lifestyle & interests (photography, gaming, fitness) and life stage (college leavers, job seekers).

Oracle Data Cloud (BlueKai Marketplace)

BlueKai Marketplace[54], operated by Oracle Data Cloud, is a leading global third-party data exchange. It is a gateway to Oracle's proprietary Data Cloud Audiences, B2B Audience data marketplace, as well as a host of branded data vendors. Oracle Data Cloud, positioned as a Data-as-a-Service product, is powered by Oracle ID Graph (a proprietary cross-device solution) and offers tools for combining, analyzing, and activating data from a broad range of sources.

Oracle Data Cloud Audiences comprise AddThis audiences (online intent and behavioral data), Curated audiences (multiple-source combined audiences), DLX (or Datalogix) audiences (offline purchase-based data), and Oracle Data Cloud audiences (custom and proprietary data, coming from the BlueKai exchange network itself).

Oracle Data Cloud Audiences are generally organized around industry verticals, which might span one or more of the Audiences services. For example, an automotive client can take advantage of AddThis data, with 400+ in-market segments covering car brands, classes, etc. In addition, they can use Curated audiences sourced and combined from Oracle's partner data providers, covering over 50 million car purchase intenders targetable by make, model, class, or buyer type. Finally, an automotive client might be also interested in very granular offline data (supplied by Polk/IHS Markit) offered via Datalogix. In addition to the data itself, Oracle supports their Data Cloud clients with dedicated teams of experts, specializing in all major verticals.

Oracle B2B Audience data marketplace is a solution aimed at B2B marketers, providing over 400 million business profiles and the ability to target 1 million US companies. The data is built from Oracle's proprietary sources, as well as from leading B2B data providers such as Bombora or Dun & Bradstreet.

80+ Branded data vendors are present in the BlueKai Marketplace as well, including the likes of Acxiom, comScore, Experian, Lotame, Kantar Media, or Visa Audiences. Each data provider offers a unique blend of reach and quality, so clients need to do their own analysis and testing to discover who can deliver the highest return on advertising spend. A data hotline is available as well, to help clients identify the best segments in their context.

BlueKai Marketplace is integrated with a broad array of digital ecosystem players, including DMPs, DSPs, ad exchanges, ad servers, attribution tools, optimization tools, or social media, so that data can be used either within or outside of the Oracle ad stack.

PushSpring

PushSpring[55] offers mobile targeting data for iOS/Android, collected via PushSpring SDK and available via the PushSpring Audience Console. Using the Console, clients can combine attributes such as app ownership, persona, demographic, or language to build their own custom audience segment. PushSpring Personas are particularly interesting, using machine learning to group users by life stages (such as new parents, dog owners, or mid-life crisis), interests & activities (e.g. foodies, hardcore gamers, or casual investors), and intent (vacation shoppers, auto shoppers, etc.). Segments created on the PushSpring Audience Console can be pushed to a number of platforms for activation, and thanks to cross-device matching they can be used for desktop targeting as well.

Retargetly

Based in Buenos Aires, Argentina, Retargetly[56] is a DMP and data exchange focused on Latino and Hispanic audiences. Covering more than 150 million unique users/month in Latin America, the US, and Europe, audience segments include demography (gender, age, language, socio-economic standing), interests (such as sports, motherhood, etc.), and purchase intent (e.g. cars, plane tickets). Retargetly segments are available through many of the major DMPs, DSPs, and other platforms. Custom integrations are possible as well.

Semasio

Semasio[57], a Hamburg-based data vendor, uses a semantic profiling approach to build audience segments. The company analyzes content of webpages consumed by internet users, to create large, weighted keyword cloud profiles. With the help of machine-learning based natural language processing, Semasio builds standardized as well as custom segments. Standard segments (referred to as "Classic Targets") include socio-demographics (gender, age, job status, education, etc.), interests (such as automobile, career, gossip, or B2B), and purchase intent (e.g. loans, travel, sporting goods). Semasio also provides look-a-like modeling on a defined segment to create an audience of "Semantic Twins".

Skimlinks

Skimlinks[58] helps publishers monetize their content by automatically turning product links into trackable affiliate links. This enables both affiliate income, as well as capture of commercially valuable data for an additional revenue stream. Skimlinks has a network of 57,000 publishers with over 1.5 million websites, giving it the scale for user segmentation. Audience segments are all focused on purchase intent, but vary in the degree of immediacy. "Affinity" segments are interested in a brand (read about it repeatedly), while "Wants to buy" show more eagerness – having read content and clicked repeatedly on links related to a brand or a topic. Finally, "About to buy" are users who are actively in-market shopping for a given category.

TruSignal

TruSignal[59] is a US-based data provider, using offline data and a predictive scoring platform to segment 220 million US adults. Data is collected from public records, surveys, service records, local listings, and other sources. TruSignal offers a selection of predictive audiences, custom audiences, audience expansion/look-a-like modeling, and specialized audiences (including auto, business, financial services, or politics). Clients can build their own segments using the TruSignal Platforms, which is integrated with DSPs, DMPs, and other platforms.

V12 Data

V12 Data[60] aggregates, segments, and activates data across online and offline channels. Digital audiences are built from offline data (including demographics, lifestyle, auto, purchase, CPG, B2B), and comprise 1,900+ segments in 15 categories. V12 Data segments include CPG audiences by category, mover segments (such as pre-movers or new movers), automotive audiences, finance, travel, PYCO personality profiles, sports & fitness, or demographics.

Visa Audiences

Visa Audiences[61] are based on $3 trillion worth of ano-nymized purchase data generated from U.S. Visa credit cards. Consumers are segmented by merchant category, frequency of spend, time of day, spend amount, or offline vs. online spend. Categories include retail, automotive, grocery, technology, travel, or seasonal expenditures. 175 pre-built audience segments are available, but clients can also request custom solutions. Visa Audiences are integrated with major DMPs, data exchanges, and other ecosystem players.

VisualDNA

VisualDNA[62], owned by Nielsen, gathers data from opt-in visual personality quizzes, to create rich psychographic user profiles. To increase scale, VisualDNA uses look-a-like modeling. Audience segments span demograph-ics, auto, entertainment, or finance, and are available internationally (including the UK, the US, France, Spain, Germany, or Italy).

Webbula

Webbula[63] offers exclusively non-modeled, determin-istic data gathered from over 100 sources including publisher partners, transaction data, surveys, municipal records, online and offline directories, or registrations. Using proprietary "CloudHygiene" and "WebbuScore" technologies, data is checked against fraud and scored for accuracy. Data segments, covering over 340 million cookies and more than 200 million mobile IDs, include demographics (e.g. age, gender, net worth, education, income), automotive data (year, make, model, body style, etc.), B2B data (company characteristics, industry, premium data), political data (voters and donors), financial data (savings, investments, credit, insurance), and interest data.

Ziff Davis

With a publisher portfolio including IGN, PCMag, Geek, Everyday Health, AskMen, or TechBargains, Ziff Davis[64] is a global media company specializing in consumer and business technology, gaming, entertainment, healthcare, shopping, and men's lifestyle. Audience segments, covering 102 million monthly users, 500+ topics, and available across 114 countries, are built with data sourced primarily from browsing activity on owned and operated websites, as well as subscriptions or ecommerce events. Audience segments categories include consumer electronics, men's lifestyle, gaming & entertainment, business & information technology, mobile phones & plans, and software.

Chapter 5 Introduction to data management platforms

Data management platform (DMP) is a complex piece of software used to collect, store, classify, analyze, and distribute large quantities of data. It is a cornerstone technology for larger organizations when it comes to advertising data management, with rapidly increasing adoption. Given both their importance and complexity, full two chapters of this book are dedicated to DMPs. This chapter will give a general overview of the most important aspects and capabilities, broadly grouped into data collection, data classification, analysis & reporting, data modeling, data distribution, implementation & user rights management, cross-device, and privacy regulation compliance. Chapter 6 will then follow up with profiles of top DMP vendors.

Data collection

Data collection is a core capability of every data management platform. Being able to pull data from various disparate sources into one place may unlock enormous value. Typically, DMPs can ingest first-party data, second-party data from contracted partners, as well as third-party data from external providers.

What differentiates various DMPs is the range of available data sources and integrations out of the box, data collection implementation, and speed of data transfer. The best DMPs have a large number of reliable (ideally lossless) and fast data integrations with other technology and data vendors. In addition, they offer an easy implementation with customization options.

First-party data ingestion

First-party data is collected directly from DMP client's own users. Usually, this data is collected from client websites, ad campaigns, mobile apps, CRM systems, search campaigns, social media, email communication, or offline sources. With the wide array of data sources falling under the first-party category umbrella, together with the diverse capabilities and designs of data management platforms, there is no universal method of collecting this data.

Website data is usually gathered by placing a DMP tag on each page, which sends structured data into the DMP when the page is loaded. This data is tied to a user identifier (e.g. cookie ID or a hashed login), so that the DMP can file it correctly. Website data might include for example page URL, title, referrer, search keyword (used to get to the site, or in an on-site search), page keywords, or custom data points. The DMP tag can also send technical data, such as browser type, operating system, browser language, or geo location.

Mobile app data is collected using a DMP-specific software development kit (SDK), commonly offered for iOS and Android. Offline data from a structured database, such as a CRM system, is often ingested by uploading a file formatted to the DMP specifications (in a process called data onboarding, as discussed in Chapter 2). Ad Campaign data, including impressions, clicks, and other events, is typically captured by inserting a piece of code (also called a "pixel") into campaign creatives. This code then sends campaign data into the DMP. Alternatively, the DMP can ingest a log file from the ad server used to deliver a campaign.

These are just some examples of how a DMP might go about ingesting first-party data from the most common sources. More advanced DMPs provide APIs to simplify data collection and transfer. The exact implementation will depend on the particular DMP design

and partner integrations, as well as client data ingestion requirements. As each client has a different technology stack, it is important to make sure the DMP can
integrate well with the critical data sources – ideally, the
DMP and data source/vendor should have a ready-made
integration available which can be easily customized and
deployed.

Second-party data ingestion

Second-party data is obtained through partnerships with
other entities, and is essentially their first-party data. This
is often facilitated via data exchanges, built directly into
the data management platform. An integrated data exchange lets a DMP client easily set up data deals with
selected partners, without having to worry about data
transfer, contracts, or billing. These data exchanges usually allow some degree of flexibility as to how deals are
structured – variables can include pricing model (flat
fee or CPM), usage (modeling/targeting/analytics), or
privacy (public vs. private deal). To take advantage of an
integrated data exchange to share second-party data,
both the buyer and the seller typically need to be clients
of the same DMP.

Alternatively, second-party data can be shared
through a custom integration outside of a data exchange.
Data itself is transferred in a similar fashion to first-party data (by implementing data buyer's DMP tag on the

seller's website, for example). The two partners need to sign a contract and manage billing themselves.

Third-party data ingestion

Third-party data is obtained from external providers, who have no direct partnership with the buyer. DMPs typically have a long list of pre-integrated third-party data vendors, so there is no need for a complicated and lengthy integration process. Some data management platforms, such as Oracle BlueKai or Lotame, even offer their own proprietary data. Of the three data sources, third-party data is the most standardized and easiest to incorporate.

Data classification

Once data enters a data management platform, it needs to be organized. This is achieved with the help of either standardized or custom taxonomies, data classification rules, and special tools to facilitate the process.

Taxonomy provides a logical way of structuring data, making it easy to work with later on. For example, a taxonomy might contain different folders for purchase intent, interest, and sociodemographic data. One level deeper within the purchase intent folder, a car manufacturer might have a "new car" folder. Within it, there could be individual car brands, models, etc. Each client is working with different data, so a good DMP should allow for plenty of customization. While some DMPs let their clients create custom taxonomies from scratch, others include standardized taxonomies with some customization options. A standardized taxonomy makes it easy to get started and share data within the wider ecosystem. On the other hand, it might not fit the client's needs, and could make the DMP interface needlessly complex.

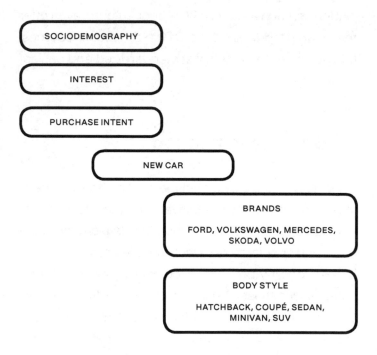

FIGURE 5: TAXONOMY EXAMPLE

With a taxonomy in place, we can start collecting actual data using segment rules. Let us say we want to create a segment of recent frequent visitors to www. AdTechResearch.com. A sample rule might look something like this:

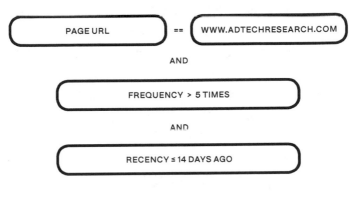

FIGURE 6: SAMPLE CLASSIFICATION RULE

A good DMP allows for a lot of flexibility when it comes to creating segment rules. Typically, one can use standard comparison operators (such as ==, !=, <, >=, etc.), and other, DMP specific operators (e. g. "contains" or "starts with"). Rules can often be combined into more complex expressions using Boolean operators AND, OR, and NOT. Each DMP works differently with segment rules, and uses a different nomenclature. In general, the more flexible segment definitions can be the better. While most DMPs require manual segment definition, some can do it automatically as well.

A great DMP lets the client work efficiently with their data using bulk tools and/or APIs. While it is fairly easy to create a few segment rules manually in the user interface, it is a whole different story creating and maintaining thousands (or tens of thousands) of them. Depending on client's requirements and planned usage, bulk data management tools could be critical. These tools can be used to create, edit, or delete segment rules or the taxonomy – thousands of items at a time.

Analysis & reporting

Collecting and classifying data is all good and well, but the real power of a DMP lies in being able to extract actual value from it. Part of this value is understanding the data (and people behind it). This understanding can be pretty basic (e.g. segment size over time), intermediate (such as segment profiling using overlaps with external data), or fairly complex (uncovering new segments using look-a-like modeling, which will be covered separately in the next section). DMPs differ a great deal in the analytical tools they offer out of the box, without the need to crunch the data in a third-party tool.

Reporting is the most basic use case for DMP analytics tools. It is important to know what the segment composition is, how many users belong to each segment (on a daily, weekly, or a monthly basis), and how many of these can actually be targeted in a live campaign. Trends are critical as well – some segments can be very seasonal (or one-time events, typical for sports), others are very stable (demographics). Most DMPs should be able to provide such data, but they differ in presentation within the UI and export/integration options if a third-party tool such as Tableau[65] is to be used for reporting. Ideally a customizable dashboard should be available, with a number of (scheduled or ad-hoc) export options.

An important and very useful analytical technique is audience profiling. In essence, we look at the overlaps and affinity of a chosen segment against other segments to determine its profile. For example, we can discover high overlap between a segment of IT professionals and users of Linux operating system. This is valuable for at least three reasons – we can better understand our target segment, discover related segments, and compare segments against each other or the general population. What makes audience profiling really exciting is the use of second- and third-party data in addition to first-party data. With it, new and previously unavailable insights can be gained, and valuable targeting opportunities uncovered. For example, we can verify our data against another source, profile target segments against previously unknown characteristics, or expand targeting to similar segments from external sources. Another interesting option is profiling against conversion segments (i.e. segments which indicate that a conversion or other high-value event occurred). This way, segments can be compared against each other to optimize a campaign or determine their value. While it is common to offer some kind of an audience profiling tool, DMPs differ in things such as minimum segment size, ease of use, or visual representation. Some DMPs also offer profiling against data sources in addition to other segments.

A separate set of specialized tools is used for campaign analytics across all stages of the campaign. Even before a campaign is live, some DMPs can run a pre-campaign analysis to determine which segments are most likely to perform well (this is essentially a special case of segment profiling). Once the campaign has started, its performance can be monitored across basic measures such as impressions, clicks, conversions, or other events. This performance can then be analyzed by segment, which in turn enables optimization. More of the budget is allocated to segments performing well, while poor performers are eliminated from the campaign. After the campaign has ended, a performance report (either visual or in the form of a data table) can summarize results across the entire funnel – from segments targeted through impressions, clicks, all the way to conversions. This can be used to learn what works and what does not for the sake of future campaigns. Some DMPs might also offer an optimal frequency report, which shows the ideal ratio between number of impressions served per user and conversions. This helps to fine tune campaigns by placing a frequency cap at the right number of impressions.

For DMP users who sell their data to other parties, special reports may exist to monitor this revenue stream. In some cases (when for instance the DMP is part of a full-stack solution including a demand-side platform), data usage reports might be available. This report can highlight things like total revenue generated from selling data, or number of impressions when it was used – broken down by advertiser/agency, date, etc. Often times though the DMP is not directly connected to the campaign delivery technology, so it has no visibility of these measures. In such a case, a data seller has to rely on self-reporting by the data buyer for billing purposes.

Testing and verifying various hypotheses is a staple of modern digital marketing. Some DMPs therefore offer tools which enable easy A/B testing. For instance, a segment can be randomly divided into several mutually exclusive test segments, including a control group. These new test segments can be run against each other to gauge performance of different destinations, creatives, etc. This can be extremely valuable for performance marketers, or clients seeking continuous optimization.

Data modeling

A good DMP should offer the possibility of data modeling (also known as look-a-like modeling or audience extension), either built-in, or through an integrated vendor. This functionality enables advertisers to achieve much larger scale while maintaining targeting accuracy.

Data modeling works by algorithmically finding users with similar behaviors or characteristics to a given segment. These newly discovered users can then be targeted or otherwise used, either as part of the same segment (audience extension) or in a separate segment. This process requires a very large user pool, with sufficient amount of data points for each user.

In order to run a data model in a DMP, we must usually select the underlying segment, look-back time interval (typically 7, 30 or more days), algorithm to be used, and naturally data to be used for modeling. The underlying segment is normally taken from first-party data, and can be any group valuable to the advertiser – for instance users who have converted on their site, or who belong to a certain audience segment. It is important to choose the right look-back time interval. 1-7 days might be suitable for modeling purchase intent, while 30 or more days would work better for sociodemographic profiling. If a DMP vendor offers multiple modeling algorithms (often from third parties), it is best to try a few and run a test to see which one performs the best. And finally, it is good to be able to choose which data pool is to be used for modeling. We might not want to use all of the data available in a DMP (for data ownership or other reasons), or we might wish to take advantage of external data.

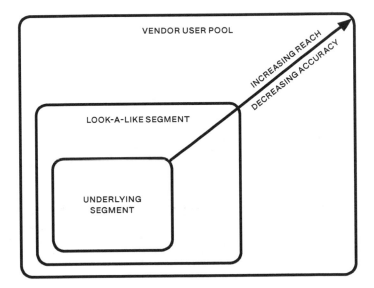

FIGURE 7: LOOK-A-LIKE MODELING

A model is usually not run in real time, but in DMP specific time frame/interval. This ranges from hours to several days. Once the model has run, DMP will report the results. Model quality will depend on data and algorithm used, size of the underlying segment, and other factors. There is usually a negative non-linear correlation between the reach and the accuracy of a model. It is great for an analyst to be able to choose whether they prefer high accuracy/similarity and lower reach, the opposite, or any other point on the model curve.

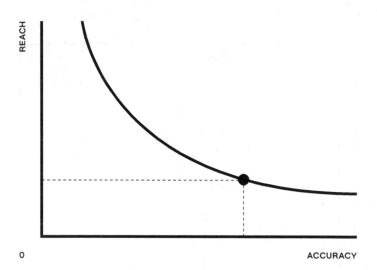

FIGURE 8: REACH VS. ACCURACY OF A MODEL

It is also helpful if the DMP UI shows which data points were most important in the final model, as this helps to confirm its validity. To maintain freshness of the model, it needs to be re-run on a regular basis – this is usually done automatically by the DMP.

An interesting possibility for data modeling is the use of third- or second-party data. This can be particularly valuable if a DMP client does not have a large pool of their own first-party data to model on, or if external data vendors have very relevant audiences which are hard to acquire or discover directly. A special deal needs to be agreed with an external data vendor for this use case.

Data modeling is a fantastic DMP feature, that can deliver a lot of value for certain advertisers. However, it is not a silver bullet when it comes to ad targeting. A lot of testing and fine-tuning is necessary to arrive at a model which delivers good results, and often the models simply do not work – because the resulting user pool is either too small or too inaccurate.

Data activation

We have already seen how a DMP can create value in several ways, particularly through better understanding of the data and users behind it, and discovering new targeting opportunities algorithmically. Now it is time to bring this value home and take action on data. For the most part, this happens outside of a DMP itself by deploying data to satisfy client needs and business goals. These commonly include ad targeting, site content customization, analytics, or selling data to generate additional revenue.

It is important for a DMP to have high-quality data integrations with the vendors and distribution destinations the client is planning to use. Here, full-stack solutions can have an upper hand, if you are planning to use both DMP and data destinations from the same stack. Typically, data transfer would be very quick with minimum data loss, along with a trivial setup. However, standalone DMP solutions are not necessarily worse in this regard, as long as the vendor offers high-quality integration with your preferred data destination. Ideally, this would be a real-time server-to-server integration (data is transferred continually between DMP and destination servers as it is generated, i.e. synchronously). Other options include batch server-to-server (data is transferred in larger batches in regular intervals, i.e. asynchronously), pixel-based transfer (synchronous but adds a lot of unnecessary pixels to the page), or writing data directly to browser cookies.

Perhaps the most common use case for DMP data is ad targeting. This usually involves data transfer into one or multiple DSPs or ad servers. Nature of the targeting data will determine the required data integration quality. If the data is scarce and valuable (such as data used for retargeting, which usually represents imminent purchase intent), any lag or data loss will have negative impact on the campaign. On the other hand, if the data is more plentiful and relatively stable over time (e.g. demographic data), some delay and data loss in transfer is not a big deal.

Site content customization is another popular use case for DMP data, particularly for publishers. This can be achieved through direct integration between the DMP and a content management system (CMS) to share a user profile. If this is not possible, a common workaround is using browser cookies whereby the DMP writes data into a browser cookie. Let us say the user is classified as a huge sports fan in the DMP. When a page is being rendered, the CMS evaluates the user profile (or a publisher's server reads the cookie) and customizes the page with lots of sports content. Although this particular implementation example sounds very straightforward, using data for content customization is not at all trivial. There needs to be a robust logic in the background to determine which content should be displayed in which case (a user can be for example a huge sports fan, a car buff, and a heavy reader of the business section at the same time), so that the publisher maximizes the time spent on site and thus generates more advertising revenue.

DMP data can be used to generate new insights and regular reports. This can be accomplished either within the DMP user interface using built-in analytics and reporting tools, or by exporting data into more advanced platforms (such as Tableau or GoodData[66]).

Many DMP clients create an additional revenue stream by selling their data. This is often done through marketplaces which are built directly into the DMP. Some DMPs collect data into standardized taxonomies, and sell it on their client's behalf. Selling custom data is a bit trickier and requires not only an integration with the destination, but often a special contract with the purchasing party and a reporting/billing agreement.

As we have seen, there are many applications for DMP data. A typical DMP client would be pushing data to multiple destinations across a wide range of activities. This can quickly become confusing and difficult to manage, so a well-designed user interface is key. It should be easy to get an overview of which data (folders, segments, etc.) is being pushed to which destinations and through which integration method. These integrations also need to be easy to configure without the need of client service, and pause/resume according to current needs. The aim of a good data distribution management interface is to empower the DMP client to precisely control the flow of data, which is critical not only from a business perspective, but also with regard to privacy and data protection regulations.

Implementation & user rights management

Successfully implementing a data management platform is always a challenge. DMPs differ in their implementation approach, the level of client support throughout the process, and availability of certified partners who can help in each market. Once the DMP is up and running, specialists on the client side are needed to take advantage of it on day-to-day basis. Ease of use, training, and a thorough documentation are therefore necessary to overcome the usually steep learning curve.

Most of the implementation work consists in integrating data sources for ingestion, building a taxonomy and data collection rules, creating segments, and finally integrating data distribution channels.

As we have seen above, each data source requires a different ingestion method, and these further vary by DMP vendor. What is always important though is that the DMP vendor has a pre-existing integration with the required data source, as building it from scratch can be a very time-consuming process. If the integration already exists, all that is needed is customizing and testing it for each particular implementation. Setting up data ingestion is where the DMP client service team or a local partner can (and often must) help the most.

Once data starts flowing into the DMP, a taxonomy, data collection rules, and segments have to be created. What it entails is covered in detail in a previous section. From the implementation perspective though, this can easily take the most time, and possibly become a never-ending process with constant improvements and maintenance. A DMP client service team can help, but it is best if the client at least provides design. Ideally the taxonomy and rules should be built and maintained in-house, to provide maximum control and flexibility.

Integrating data activation channels is analogous to integrating data sources for ingestion, and is covered in a separate section as well. DMPs differ in what integrations and data marketplaces they offer out of the box, so it is important to pick the right one to simplify implementation. Using a DMP as a part of a full-stack solution can make the implementation a bit easier (particularly the integration parts), but it could have other downsides depending on the vendor.

If the DMP is going to be shared by multiple people, departments, or even business entities, user rights management becomes an important issue. A DMP should allow for a lot of flexibility and rights levels to create and manage roles that fit the client's needs. Typical roles include admin (with read/write/edit access to everything), user (with restricted rights) and read-only user with limited visibility. It should be possible to define user roles both by what they can do, as well as where they can do it. Access can be for example restricted based on segments, folders, data sources, geography, destinations, etc. It is therefore important to plan ahead who and how is going to be using the DMP – otherwise an admin might end up pulling reports for colleagues who cannot get the right level of access, which is a waste of resources.

Cross-device

Cross-device integration involves the identification of users across their devices/browsers, and subsequent use of a unified profile and related data. Data management platforms, being the central user-level data hubs, can be very helpful in building cross-device profiles.

Out of the box, DMPs tend to collect the bulk of their data on a device/browser level with the help of cookies on desktop and device IDs on mobile. However, one device or browser may be used by multiple users, and a single user would often use multiple devices and browsers. How do we know that a particular laptop, tablet, and a mobile phone belong to the same person – and thus the data from these devices should be pooled together? Or say we want to target a particular user (who shows a high purchase intent for our product) across all of her devices – how should we accomplish this? The solutions to these and similar problems fall under "cross-device" umbrella.

There are two basic approaches to identifying a user on multiple devices – probabilistic and deterministic. The deterministic approach takes advantage of a unique, persistent ID – such as a login or an email address. This guarantees reliable user identification resistant to cook- ie deletion or third-party cookie blocking, but such an ID is not always available (generally this would require for a user to be constantly logged in). Some DMPs can work with unique IDs (in a hashed, non-PII form) to build a deterministic cross-device profile. Since most clients would only have a limited pool of first-party deterministic user IDs, some DMPs allow their clients to share these to increase scale. Probabilistic approach works different- ly – the method consists in analyzing vast quantities of data (such as device type, browser, operating system, IP address, location, etc.) to merge user profiles based on statistical probability. Some DMPs offer a probabilistic cross-device solution, often through a third-party vendor (such as screen6[67] or TAPAD[68]).

The cross-device solution can be a key factor when choosing a DMP vendor. A client with a lot of logged-in us- ers might find a lot of value in deterministic solution, while a client whose users generally do not log in could benefit from a probabilistic one. Also, it is not always necessary or welcome to use cross-device profiles – a good DMP should be therefore flexible and let their clients decide for which applications they have cross-device turned on, and for which they would still be using un-merged device/browser level data.

Privacy regulation compliance

With ever-growing regulation to protect user rights, privacy is becoming an increasingly important concern for DMP vendors and their clients.

DMPs in general do not allow the collection of personally identifiable information (PII) – this is data that can either alone, or in combination with other data, identify a real person. Data such as name, address, social security/passport/national ID number, credit card numbers, phone number, or date of birth typically fall under PII. DMPs usually prohibit sending such data into the system in the client contract, and also conduct random checks to delete PII if discovered.

A good DMP vendor would not only comply with privacy regulations (such as GDPR) and help solve compliance on their clients' behalf, but should also have robust data protection and security measures in place. Data needs to be stored and processed safely, to minimize risk of data theft or leakage. A well-designed data processing system in the background, as well as data distribution management within the UI, will go a long way in retaining control of the data flow.

Chapter 6
DMP vendors

We have seen what data management platforms can do – this chapter will now introduce the top DMP vendors. Each DMP has a different history, positioning, strategy, capabilities, regional presence, customer service levels, and naturally pricing. These are just some of the factors a potential customer might consider, but there are many more that might play a significant role. Without a doubt, DMP selection is a very complex process.

This overview of top vendors is intended as a starting point for creating a shortlist and embarking on initial conversations. Digital advertising professionals might also find it beneficial to get a good grasp of who the main players in this space are, and what they can offer. In an alphabetical order, profiles of Adform DMP, Adobe Audience Manager, The Adex, Amobee DMP, Google Audience Center 360, Lotame DMP, MediaMath DMP, Neustar IDMP, Nielsen DMP, Oracle BlueKai, Salesforce DMP, and Zipline by KBM Group follow.

Adform DMP

Adform[69] is a relative newcomer to the data management platform space, originally focusing on ad serving and a demand-side platform. Although it has offered a simple DMP functionality for a while, this product has since 2014 become a top priority. With rapid improvement and the necessary investment, technologies, and know-how to back it up, Adform is now offering an enterprise-level DMP on par with many traditional vendors. Adform offers the only DMP in the market with an advertising background – so speed, processing huge amounts of data, and collecting advertising metrics comes very naturally to the company.

To make the day-to-day DMP management easier, everything is API accessible. Adform offers a cross-device identity solution that can be utilized with the DMP, and combines deterministic and probabilistic approach. Additional features include look-a-like modeling, and visually attractive data analysis tools (such as overlap and affinity reports).

Adform is very serious about data security and privacy regulations compliance. The DMP is GDPR ready, and is data security certified to ISO/IEC 27001. Adform DMP runs on proprietary servers rather than the cloud, making it easier to comply with data protection laws. In addition, it is also MRC accredited for viewability mea-surement, which is unique among DMP vendors.

With an ad server and a DSP in the stack, Adform DMP will work out-of-the box for advertisers and agen-cies who aim to use data mainly for ad targeting. On top, other DMP functionalities like onsite personalization and deep integration into enterprise-grade (e.g. Adobe) analytics systems for marketing automation scenarios are of course also possible.

Adform DMP caters not only to advertisers and agencies, but also to publishers. Publishers can use it to monetize their data as either second- or third- party. There is a private marketplace to sell data, with full control over pricing and visibility of all data transactions. Adform DMP takes care of the billing and contracts on its plat-form, making it easy to get started. As such, publishers can take advantage of the data marketplace, and benefit from the DMP's focus on regulations compliance. At the end, Advertisers can access a global data marketplace to purchase third-party data for their campaigns.

The DMP is part of an integrated ad stack solution called "Advertiser Edge", including a demand-side plat-form, ad server, and creative platform. Even though it perfectly runs as a standalone solution, for a client using other parts of the stack, the benefits that come on top include better usability, smooth workflow, and efficiency.

To illustrate, being part of a single ad stack means that there is no data loss and minimum latency when using Adform DSP for targeted media buying. This can be very valuable if a client aims to rely heavily on retargeting, or other time-sensitive storytelling or targeting strategies.

Adobe Audience Manager

Adobe Audience Manager (AAM)[70] has been a leader of the DMP market ever since Adobe's acquisition of Demdex, enabling Adobe to get a head start in the market for integration with the Adobe digital marketing technology stack. AAM works both as a standalone product, as well as with Adobe's suite of advertising, marketing, and analytics solution called the Adobe Experience Cloud. It is truly an enterprise-level data management platform designed both for publishers as well as advertisers, handling petabytes of data while offering the best of breed capabilities for audience activation across channels. AAM has also evolved into an identity management platform with marketers now having the ability to identify customers across various personal devices.

AAM comes with a wide array of ready-made integrations for data ingestion and distribution, which are easy to customize and activate. Through a built-in "Audience Marketplace", clients can buy and sell second- and third- party data. Adobe takes data protection and privacy seriously, enabling effective data rights management and regulation compliance with in-dustry-first features such as Data Export Controls.

One of the great features of Adobe Audience Mana-ger is a very flexible taxonomy and segment creation process. The taxonomy can be completely custom to fit client needs, while segments are built on two levels – traits (basic data capture) combine into segments (where recency, frequency, and operators can be set). AAM also includes robust APIs, so it can be managed in bulk outside the UI, and is easy to integrate with other technologies.

As can be expected, the DMP contains a number of reports, including overlap between segments, or data trends over time. Advertisers have the option to also track and use campaign data (such as impressions, clicks, conversions, and other events). There is a built-In look-a-like modeling solution which performs well and can be used to extend segments or find new target au-diences. AAM also supports deterministic cross-device identification, which is great for clients who have a lot of logged-in users. Cross-device IDs can also be shared between clients through the "Marketing Cloud Device Co-op", increasing user/device recognition for clients who have fewer deterministic user IDs available.

Adobe Audience Manager is a full-fledged DMP with a lot of value creation potential in the right hands. However, it can be an overkill for smaller or less advanced clients, both in capabilities it offers as well as cost. The learning curve might be a bit steeper as well compared to simpler DMPs, so a lot of time and resources need to be dedicated to managing AAM. For the right client though, it can easily be the best DMP solution out there.

The Adex

The Adex[71] is a leading independent data management platform for marketers & publishers in Europe. It is headquartered in Germany and operates globally with a strong emphasis on the European market, focusing on providing the best possible service and custom solutions. The Adex prides itself on client support offered in local languages – and, being a local player, with no time difference. With physical servers in Germany for European clients, legal know-how, and an emphasis on data security, the Adex is well positioned to comply with strict data protection regulations in the EU. The Adex has clients both on the publisher as well as advertiser side, along with some agency clients. This DMP can be accessible to smaller clients, as it offers three standard pricing tiers with increasing levels of service, together with completely custom enterprise tier.

The taxonomy is flexible, although there are optional standard dimensions to get started. It has ready-to-use direct integrations with major ecosystem players, which are maintained and tested on a regular basis. When it comes to look-a-like modeling, both a proprietary algorithm as well as third-party modeling vendors are available. The Adex offers complete control and transparency with regard to the data pool on which modeling is done, which can be very valuable to some clients. There is a deterministic built-in approach for cross-device matching. To make it work at scale, the Adex maintains relationships with many providers of deterministic identifiers which helps their clients extend their own deterministic ID pools (and onboard their offline data with maximum match rates). There is also an option to connect to a dedicated probabilistic cross-device provider in order to expand a deterministic cross-device graph. A separate, but often complementary product to the DMP is Datanexx, a data-selling platform. It enables clients to export their data to various marketplaces on a revenue share basis. When a minimum revenue threshold is met, Datanexx is provided as a managed service with no set up cost or recurring fees.

The Adex, as a fast-growing independent player in the DMP space, is very ambitious with regards to further growth in Europe. The DMP will focus on real-time segmentation, improving look-a-like modeling, getting more partners for deterministic IDs and look-a-like data pools on board, as well as adding exchange integrations and improving these (e.g. by getting user data directly into the bid stream).

Although the Adex is not the most comprehensive DMP in terms of features, it has some of the strongest core functionalities (such as data collection, processing, and distribution) on the European market. It can be an interesting option for clients who require data protection compliance, responsive local support, custom solutions, and high-quality core DMP functionality.

Amobee (formerly Turn) DMP

Amobee DMP[72] has been rebranded following the acquisition of Turn by Amobee, a subsidiary of Singapore-based Singtel. Turn started off as a demand-side platform (DSP), but had been developing a solid data management platform (DMP) before the sale to Amobee.

One of the world's largest independent advertising platforms, Amobee unifies key programmatic channels including all major social media platforms, formats, and devices, to provide both managed and self-service clients with easy-to-use data management and media planning capabilities as well as actionable, real-time market research and proprietary audience data. Simplifying the delivery of advertising across all channels and screens, including video, display, mobile, and social, the platform includes the Amobee DSP, Amobee DMP, Brand Intelligence and DataMine technology, which converts raw data into custom audience and campaign insights, empowering marketers to make more informed decisions.

Amobee's approach centers around the Amobee ID, an anonymous user profile combining Amobee's data with clients' first-party or purchased second- and third-party data. Amobee operates "Amobee AlwaysOn Data", a proprietary data stream consisting of over 90,000 demographic, behavioral, and psychographic attributes collected across 4 billion unique browsers and devices. This data stream is available to Amobee's clients, along with a wide selection of third-party data ready to be used at any time, without the need for custom integration.

To make implementation as smooth as possible, Amobee offers Flextag, a tag management and data collection solution. Reporting and analytics are a strong point of this DMP as well. It offers both ready-made basic reports for things like segments and campaign performance, as well as custom, specialized reports which are easy to visualize. For example, the Audience Forecaster tool lets clients predict segment reach once a targeted campaign starts running. Amobee also offers more advanced data processing capabilities, including look-a-like modeling or customer journey analysis.

Similar to other DMPs, Amobee has a number of partners (reportedly 100+, ranging from inventory sources to marketing automation platforms) to distribute and activate data managed on the platform.

Amobee is a wholly owned subsidiary of Singtel, and Amobee's marketing platform is a key component of Singtel's digital transformation and future strategy. The Singtel Group's footprint reaches 640 million mobile subscribers in Asia, Africa, and Australia. Operators have a comprehensive view and understanding of their customers, similar to Google and Facebook which also boast powerful consumer data sets. Amobee's intention is to enable the ability to unlock operator's understanding of their customers across a myriad of marketing and business functions.

Amobee is a good choice for clients who value strong DMP capabilities, seamlessly integrated with a DSP for efficient data activation.

Google Audience Center 360

Google Audience Center 360 data management platform[73] is part of the Google Analytics 360 Suite alongside Google Analytics, Tag Manager, Optimize, Data Studio, Surveys, and Attribution 360. This means it can take advantage of a native integration with other products in the suite, making it easy to ingest site activity (if a client is using Google Analytics) and other first-party data. In addition to clients' proprietary data, the DMP has an out-of-the-box access to exclusive Google Audience data (including demographic, affinity, and in-market). There are also third-party data vendors integrated into the platform.

As for the features, Audience Center 360 offers overlap and frequency optimization reports, with an option to apply a global frequency cap. Segment performance in campaigns can be analyzed, and the best performing segments extended with look-a-like modeling. There is also a built-in A/B testing tool which might be helpful both to advertisers testing segment performance, as well as publishers who might be playing with content customization. Google is naturally very strong in cross-device, having a vast deterministic ID graph to work with. Together with very persistent cookies this translates into broad and accurate cross-device reach, with minimal data loss within the Google ecosystem.

Integration with other Google products is perhaps the key distinguishing feature of Audience Center 360. In addition to the in-suite solutions already mentioned, the DMP is tightly integrated with DoubleClick products (including DoubleClick Bid Manager or DoubleClick for Publishers), AdWords, Google Display Network, or YouTube. There are some integrations with other ecosystem players, but this DMP would work best for clients who are heavily invested in the Google ad stack.

Lotame DMP

Lotame[74] is a leading independent data management platform serving publishers, marketers, and agencies. It is based in the United States, with offices around the world.

Being independent and media agnostic means that Lotame has no preferred or in-stack channel to push their clients towards. Instead, the DMP offers integrations with all major DSPs, ad servers, ad exchanges, and SSPs so that clients can freely choose who they want to work with. Independence also means that Lotame is very flexible when it comes to product roadmap, so they can better adjust to client needs and requirements.

Another distinguishing feature of Lotame is focus on external data, which is manifested in several products. First, Lotame Data Exchange (LDX) is a proprietary third-party data exchange built into Lotame DMP platform, offering over 5,000 pre-packaged audience segments aggregated across Lotame partners. Interestingly, segments include smart TV audiences in addition to the common data sources. Second, Lotame offers co-branded data with trusted partners. Third, there are branded third-party data providers integrated into the DMP.

Fourth, clients can take advantage of a second-party data exchange called Lotame Syndicate. Here, data can be bought and sold either within the DMP between clients, or pushed to a DSP. And finally, for the more advanced clients, Lotame Data Stream offers unstructured continuous data flow of consumer profiles, which can be used for modeling, analytics, or other applications beyond advertising.

Naturally, Lotame enables the collection and management of first-party data from a number of sources (such as websites, apps, social, email, CRM, search, or campaign data). As one of the foundational technologies, the DMP includes a cross-device solution which combines deterministic and probabilistic approach to build a device graph. Lotame analyzes vast amounts of data signals to find likely cross-device relationships in a probabilistic way, but matches devices deterministically when unique IDs are available. There is also a look-a-like modeling solution called Lotame Audience Optimizer, which applies modeling techniques to extend and optimize campaigns to maximize a desired KPI.

As already noted, Lotame has access to TV data and audiences. Their solution, dubbed aiTV, analyzes viewing habits and preferences to build and enhance user profiles. This data can be used both to target chosen audiences on TV screen, but also to reach TV viewers on desktops, mobiles, or tablets.

Lotame is a great choice for clients who want a solid DMP, a flexible and independent vendor, highly-praised customer service, and seamless access to Lotame Data Exchange.

MediaMath DMP

MediaMath[75], a US company with a global footprint, is positioned as a one-stop programmatic execution platform across all channels, combining strong DSP and DMP capabilities.

Indeed, one of the key selling points of MediaMath DMP lies in being an integrated solution – having a DSP in the same stack, it is easy to activate any segments created in the DMP. Not only is the workflow streamlined, but data is available for targeting in real-time with no loss. Moreover, instant segment sizing in the DSP is possible, and segments used in live campaigns respond immediately to new data coming into the DMP (MediaMath calls this feature "adaptive segments"). Media data coming via the DSP can be easily combined with other sources (such as website visitor data, mobile in-app data, offline customer data) in the DMP to create unique, tactical segments. In fact, MediaMath's proprietary machine learning algorithm called "The Brain" uses both DMP and media/bid stream data to automate bidding with respect to client's goals.

MediaMath is designed as an open platform supported by APIs, so clients can build around it to suit their needs. Hundreds of integrations with data, technology, and media partners are available, along with an app store to simplify any new setups. MediaMath is proud of high match rates with many partners, Oracle in particular. When it comes to data, the DMP offers a number of options – including proprietary "MediaMath Audiences" (based on bid stream data, available in the US, APAC, LATAM, and soon in Europe) and over 75 integrated third-party data vendors. First-party data can be onboarded across many sources, as the DMP supports standard pixel- or tag-based ingestion, proprietary CRM onboarding, server-to-server integration, or mobile SDKs.

MediaMath includes a built-in cross-device solution called "ConnectedID", which uses MediaMath's signals along with the client's (or any other party's) to create a deterministic ID Graph. The cross-device solution is deterministic, but MediaMath also has a probabilistic solution for identifying users in cookie-less environments. Look-a-like modeling, performed on bid stream data, is available as well to enable audience extension.

Advanced analytics tools offered with MediaMath DMP can be valuable to many clients. For example, there is an integrated "Data Mining Console" – an analytics platform with direct access to up to 12 months of historical campaign-generated data (raw impressions, events, and attributed event logs), with tools to perform ad hoc analyzes, uncover new segments, study conversion pathways, or supply data for custom attribution models. This product is universal and allows more savvy users to write and run their own queries or to build customer reporting templates for users who do not have SQL knowledge. The DMP also enables retroactive performance analysis – any segment can be evaluated (even if not used in the actual campaign) to see how it performed. This can be in turn used as a learning for future campaigns. Standard audience insights are available as well, including segment profiling with third-party data.

Clients who appreciate a thoroughly integrated DMP and DSP solution will be happy with MediaMath DMP. With advanced analytics, proprietary and third-party audiences, native cross-device solution, open and integrated platform, as well as capable built-in machine learning algorithm to automate bidding, MediaMath DMP is a solid, top-tier offering.

Neustar IDMP (PlatformOne)

Neustar, a US-based information services provider, positions its data management platform[76] around consumer identity. Rather than calling the product a DMP, they call it an IDMP (Identity Data Management Platform) to highlight the focus on identity resolution. To Neustar, getting identity right is key, as it enables all the follow-up activities such as controlling media exposure, building a consumer journey, or media optimization.

Neustar's identity/cross-device solution is called OneID, and it is a foundational technology behind the IDMP. It links offline and online consumer identifiers from proprietary/partner sources, as well as client CRM database and online sources (such as name, address, phone number, email address, device IDs, or IP address), and gives the consumer a persistent, unique ID. This identity can then be used to market and advertise to the consumer across channels, both online and offline. As a foundational technology, it also enables accurate measurement, reporting, analysis, and attribution.

Neustar is proud of their proprietary onboarding solution, which allows clients to make the most of their CRM data within the IDMP. Thanks to Neustar's wealth of offline data, extensive partner network, and industry-leading identity resolution capabilities, onboarding guarantees maximum accuracy and high match rates.

Privacy is also an important concern. Neustar IDMP is a leading DMP in this area, handling personally identifiable information (PII) with the ultimate privacy-by-design principles.

Naturally, Neustar IDMP offers all the standard DMP features. This includes first-, second-, and third-party data ingestion, segmentation, analytics, and activation across a variety of channels (including both online and offline). The DMP also includes look-a-like functionality which facilitates audience extension.

All in all, Neustar IDMP is one of the top choices on the market today, particularly for clients who value accurate identity resolution at scale.

Nielsen DMP

Nielsen is a global market research, data, and measurement company, which entered the DMP space with its purchase of eXelate (one of the top data exchanges at the time) in 2015. Nielsen Data Management Platform is one of the key offerings within the Nielsen Marketing Cloud, sitting alongside solutions such as "Nielsen Media Impact" (media planning and optimization), "Multi-Touch Attribution" (omnichannel campaign sales attribution product), and "Journey Analytics" (path-to-purchase sales funnel analytics from live campaigns).

The key differentiating factor of Nielsen DMP is data, validated and calibrated against Nielsen's panel to ensure maximum quality. Clients get access to a treasure trove of proprietary Nielsen data, including purchase data (FMCG and Retail for example), complete cross-channel media consumption information, along with behavioral, demographic, and psychographic categories. Data is gathered across Nielsen's products (such as Nielsen Catalina Solutions, Nielsen Total Audience (TV, audio and digital data), Nielsen Buyer Insights (90% of U.S. Credit Card transactions), or newly acquired Gracenote (Smart TV viewership data across 27 million televisions world-wide), as well as other partner sources. 60,000 ready-made audience segments are available in the Nielsen DMP, but custom and modeled options are naturally also possible. Nielsen DMP brand and agency clients can gain a big advantage when permitted to use Nielsen's data for analytics, advanced modeling, and for use in oth-er applications beyond media targeting. In addition to proprietary and third-party data, Nielsen DMP includes a second-party data exchange.

Nielsen is very proud of the artificial intelligence capabilities built into the DMP. Nielsen AI powers the creation of adaptive look-a-like segments, which adjust automatically to new data flowing into the DMP in real time. Model training and validation happens on an ongo-ing basis (rather than in regularly scheduled batches) to reflect the most recent consumer behavior – this ensures that the look-a-like segment is always up to date and any communication will be relevant to the target group. Interestingly, Multi-Touch Attribution (used by majority of clients alongside the DMP) can feed data in real time into AI models, making them responsive to actual campaign performance for maximum ROI.

Taxonomy comes standardized for advertisers, publishers, and agencies, but can be completely customized as well to fit client needs. All first-party data flowing into Nielsen DMP is kept in a raw, structured format – mapping and segmentation can be done up to 30 days later. Nielsen's Device Graph, powered by Nielsen AI, employs a combination of deterministic and probabilistic approaches to cross-device, validating its 9.5 billion device IDs against Facebook to ensure accuracy.

When it comes to data activation, Nielsen is media agnostic by choice to maintain objectivity in its media measurement business. DMP clients can take advantage of around 400 integrated paid and owned media channels, including content management systems, email service providers, dynamic personalization vendors, or major programmatic platforms. Nielsen's focus is on high match rates (leading to minimal data loss) and speed (200ms refresh rates) with key partners. This ensures real time data flow, and enables cross-channel frequency and sequencing control right inside the DMP.

Finally, Nielsen is very strong in outcome measurement and attribution, since the majority of their clients use the DMP as part of the marketing cloud. Using Multi-Touch Attribution or Journey Analytics, they can provide the ROI of the DMP and all of the marketing campaigns and tactics that take advantage of it. Overall, Nielsen is a great choice for clients who can take advantage of

Nielsen's proprietary data beyond targeting, and who need an advanced AI, measurement, and attribution solution.

Oracle BlueKai

The Oracle data management platform, also known as Oracle BlueKai[77] (BlueKai was the original company Oracle acquired the DMP from), is one of the top-tier offerings in the market. It is part of Oracle's marketing cloud, which includes products such as Oracle Eloqua, Maxymiser, or Responsys.

Oracle BlueKai is a great option for clients who have a good maturity in the advertising space and look for increasing their ROI in media spend by extending their own data with external data. Oracle operates a "Data Cloud" – data marketplace comprising of vendor and third-party data. Oracle's proprietary data offering includes online interest and intent behavioral data (Oracle AddThis), offline purchase-based data (Oracle Datalogix), and so-called "Curated Audiences" which combine data (such as behavioral, interest, in-market, demographics, lifestyles, etc.) from multiple reputable sources. In addition to Oracle's data, there is a vast selection of integrated third-party data providers to pick from. Third-party data is available in real-time and immediately with no additional setup, and is free to use for analytics and look-a-like modeling. As is common with top-tier DMPs, a second-party data exchange exists on the platform to facilitate buying and selling of data among BlueKai clients and data providers.

Another distinctive feature beyond the Data Cloud is BlueKai's focus on high-quality integrations. The DMP aims to be agnostic when it comes to data activation – there are lots of ready-to-go server to server integrations, so that each client can use their preferred partners with the DMP.

Being one of the DMP market leaders, Oracle BlueKai naturally has a cross-device solution (called "Oracle ID Graph"). This periodically combines multiple ID types from Oracle ID data partners to arrive at a very accurate deterministic and probabilistic identity graph, covering the bulk of the US and international population. BlueKai also offers look-a-like modeling, either with a proprietary algorithm, or via third-party vendors.

Taxonomy is largely standardized, but custom data points (base units of data collection) can be added as well, in a self-service way building a private taxonomy (hierarchy of categories). Data points can be combined into more complex segments using Boolean logic. Apart from the standard first-, second-, and third-party data ingestion from various sources, Oracle BlueKai allows clients to collect campaign data such as impressions, clicks, and conversions. This can be used to optimize conversion funnel with the help of a funnel analysis report, or to discover new segments which can be used for targeting via an audience discovery report.

All in all, Oracle BlueKai is one of the top data management platforms, suitable mainly for enterprise clients who value access to external data and high-quality integrations with vendors outside the Oracle stack. Given the advanced user rights management, BlueKai is also an interesting proposition for agencies running a DMP on behalf of multiple clients.

Salesforce DMP

Salesforce DMP[78] is part of Salesforce Marketing Cloud, a suite of tools designed to simplify B2C and B2B marketing at scale. The DMP was until recently called Krux, and joined the Salesforce product family in a 2016 acquisition.

What makes Salesforce DMP special is their approach towards data collection and classification. Salesforce ingests all the raw, unstructured data that flows into it, so that none of it is lost. The taxonomy/data classification schema is defined with keys only, while values (and in turn data points) are derived automatically from the ingested data. This is a much more flexible approach compared to the common relational database with pre-defined keys and values, eliminating a lot of the bias an analyst doing DMP setup might introduce into the data structure. The system is also much easier to maintain, as a lot of the classification work happens automatically. Collecting all the raw data has its own benefits as well, such as access to older data which could be otherwise lost, or better look-a-like modeling performance.

Salesforce DMP features powerful machine learning capabilities, powered by the proprietary "Einstein" technology. This helps to uncover and define new valuable segments automatically based on patterns in the raw data, instead of relying on judgement of data analysts. Being an advanced DMP, Salesforce offers a cross-device identity solution which combines deterministic and probabilistic approach. To make it as accurate as possible, the overall ID graph is created algorithmically across all Salesforce DMP data. However, to make sure no client data is shared, individual ID graphs are then created for each client based on their own data. The DMP also features a look-a-like modeling solution with proprietary algorithm, which can be used for audience extension either on first-party data, or on third-party data.

The DMP naturally offers integrated third-party data via data vendors (not much proprietary data is offered, apart from geographical and similar technical data), which is available as samples for analytics and first-party data comparison. There is a second-party data marketplace as well, which can be used not only between Salesforce clients, but also with selected DSPs – all while Salesforce takes care of the reporting and billing. Clients who use the DMP for media targeting can also take advantage of impression-level data ingestion from select DSPs, and use the built-in analytics to optimize their campaigns.

To sum up, Salesforce DMP is a very advanced DMP for enterprise clients, with a unique approach to data collection and classification and a host of cutting-edge features such as Salesforce Einstein or a vast ID graph. The extensive capabilities, while fantastic for clients who can utilize them, might be too much for smaller or less advanced clients though.

Zipline (KBM Group)

KBM Group is a company within WPP (belonging to the Young & Rubicam Group under Wunderman), focusing on data collection, management, analysis, and activation on behalf of their clients. Their data management platform, called Zipline[79], is an enterprise-scale solution with global footprint.

Zipline DMP offers powerful offline data (such as a CRM database) onboarding capabilities. Their profile database covers around 95 % of the US population, yielding fairly high match rates when converting offline profiles to online audience segments. In addition to first-party data collection, the platform offers third-party vendor data (including social data ingestion via DataSift[80]). The DMP can further provide audience extension via look-a-like modeling.

When it comes to data activation, Zipline has integrations with some leading ecosystem players including DSPs, SSPs, or ad networks. Data can be used both in online channels (including email or social media) as well as hybrid/offline channels such as TV or post.

Zipline DMP can be an interesting choice particularly for WPP clients, who appreciate solid onboarding capabilities and a well-rounded DMP package.

Chapter 7
Privacy and
regulation

With the explosion of personal data collection and usage, privacy concerns have been on the rise. They stem from the fact that the general public has little knowledge of current data practices in the digital advertising industry, and almost no control over their own data. Although data is often used in ways which benefit individuals (such as personalized user experiences or more relevant advertising), this frequently happens without their consent. There is also a risk of data misuse, leakage, or theft. To amend this state of affairs, governments and industry bodies have been passing regulations and enforcing best practices to set rules for handling user data.

User privacy is a complex, dynamic, and often controversial topic. It involves not only legal and ethical, but also technical aspects which can sometimes become too abstract for effective regulation. This is evidenced in the controversy over the proposed ePrivacy Regulation, where a well-intentioned attempt to strengthen privacy protection might break the current advertising-supported business model of many publishers and threaten the open digital ecosystem.

There is no doubt that personal data ownership is a precious asset, especially if the information is unique, valuable, and on a large scale. In the current state of the data ecosystem, most of it is owned or controlled by relatively few private companies[81]. However, it should be primarily the data subjects (i.e. people) who understand, own, and control their data. The trend, as set for example by GDPR in the EU and DAA's self-regulatory principles, is towards more transparency and individual control over how data is collected and used. It is important to set fundamental, and if possible stable rules for the data economy, in order to build consumer trust and define a clear playing field for the industry.

The European Union is at the forefront of user privacy protection and regulation. General Data Protection Regulation (GDPR), enforceable from May 25th, 2018, offers high transparency and privacy control standards for the EU residents. Another prominent EU privacy law is the ePrivacy Directive, to be superseded by a very controversial ePrivacy Regulation. Due to the profound impact of GDPR, ePrivacy Directive and potentially ePrivacy Regulation on the digital advertising industry data practices, more detailed overviews of the regulations follow later in this chapter.

Unlike in the EU, there is no single, comprehensive federal law regulating the collection and use of personal data in the United States[82]. Instead, data collection and usage in digital advertising is regulated by many separate federal, state, and municipal laws, as well as self-regulation[83]. The Federal Trade Commission Act (15 U.S.C. §§41-58) prohibits unfair or deceptive practices, and has been applied to both offline and online privacy and data security policies[84]. Children's Online Privacy Protection Act (15 U.S.C. §§6501-6506), discussed in more detail below, is another federal regulation focused on the collection of personal information of children under 13 years of age. Other examples of federal laws with impact on privacy include the Financial Services Monetization Act (15 U.S.C. §§6801-6827), the Health Insurance Portability and Accountability Act (HIPPA) (42 U.S.C. §1301 et seq.), the Fair Credit Reporting Act (15 U.S.C. §1681), the Electronic Communications Privacy Act (18 U.S.C. §2510) and the Computer Fraud and Abuse Act (18 U.S.C. §1030)[85]. Many laws exist on the state level, with California at the forefront of privacy regulation. The California Online Privacy Protection Act has its own section further on.

In addition to governmental regulation, industry self-regulatory practices have been developed to promote trust, knowledge, and control of individuals with regard to the digital advertising industry. The Digital

Advertising Alliance Self-Regulatory Program is the most prominent, and will be looked at in more detail below.

General Data Protection Regulation

General Data Protection Regulation (GDPR) is a regulation aimed at strengthening and harmonizing data protection in the EU, enforceable from May 25th, 2018. It applies to both EU companies, as well as foreign companies processing data of EU residents – hence, it has a profound impact on the digital advertising data ecosystem.

GDPR requires that any data processing is lawful (i.e. meeting at least one of the specified conditions)[86]. The majority of digital advertising data will have to be processed based on explicit consent of the data subject. A record of the consent must be kept, including the exact wording, date, and means of obtaining it. Special protection is awarded to children under 16 years old – consent from their parents or guardians is required. Conditions for obtaining consent are relatively strict, including for example:

- The request for consent must be prominent and easy to understand.
- There must be a positive opt in which requires action (no default pre-ticked boxes).

- The consent cannot be a precondition of service.
- The consent must be easy to withdraw.
- The purpose of data processing needs to be declared.
- All organizations relying on the consent must be named.

As for scope, GDPR applies to personal data – any information relating to an identified or identifiable natural person[87]. Personal identifiers may include name, address, email, IP address, IDs (e.g. cookie ID, device ID), location data, photo, medical information, etc. Under GDPR, individuals have the following rights:

- To be informed (i.e. receive fair data processing information)
- To access (obtaining confirmation of personal data processing and access to it)
- To rectification (if data is inaccurate or incomplete)
- To erasure (particularly if an individual withdraws consent)
- To restriction of processing (data may be stored, but not processed)
- To data portability (i.e. obtaining personal data and using it elsewhere)

- To objection (to data processing based on legitimate interests, for direct marketing, or for research purposes)
- Rights in relation to automated decision making and profiling (i.e. protection against the risk of significant, automated decisions)

GDPR differentiates between data processors and data controllers. While the controller determines purposes and means of processing personal data, processors are responsible for the data processing itself. Both controllers and processors need to comply with GDPR principles, and must ensure (contractually where applicable) that personal data is adequately protected – for example against unlawful/unauthorized processing or loss. Prior to any new data processing activity (including adopting new technology, risky or sensitive data processing, or user profiling), data controllers are required to carry out an impact assessment[88]. Some organizations, such as those conducting large-scale behavioral tracking used in digital advertising, need to also appoint Data Protection Officers. DPOs are responsible for compliance with GDPR and other data protection laws.

Under GDPR, international data transfer outside of the EU is restricted to make sure adequate level of protection is afforded to individuals' data. Organizations are required to report more risky data breaches, either to a supervisory authority only, or also to affected individuals.

To ensure compliance, GDPR empowers data pro-tection authorities with the power of levying significant fines – up to € 20,000,000 or 4 per cent of a company's annual global turnover (whichever is higher)[89].

GDPR regulation, despite the cost and administrative burden it places on organizations processing data, has been generally well received by the industry. It provides more awareness and control for individuals, increasing their trust towards the digital advertising industry and the publishers and services it helps to support. This regulation also increases transparency of data flow, processing, and visibility of organizations involved. Together with the unification of data protection regulation across the EU, these improvements make life easier for all digital advertising industry participants.

ePrivacy Directive and ePrivacy Regulation

Directive on privacy and electronic communications (Directive 2002/58/EC, commonly known as ePrivacy Directive), regulates several aspects of the digital advertising industry, including the use of cookies in particular.

The ePrivacy Directive mandates that "to store information or to gain access to information stored in the terminal equipment of a subscriber or user is only allowed on condition that the subscriber or user concerned is provided with clear and comprehensive information... about the purposes of the processing, and is offered the right to refuse such processing by the data controller." Consent is thus generally required when using cookies for data collection and other digital advertising purposes. Consent acquisition is typically implemented via (omnipresent and immensely unpopular) cookie banners.

ePrivacy Directive, albeit controversial, is still relatively mild compared to the proposed ePrivacy Regulation which might replace it. As of writing of this book, the legislative process has not been completed, so final provisions and enforcement date is not clear. Unlike the current ePrivacy Directive which requires users to provide consent for cookies and similar technologies on each website the user visits, the Regulation proposes that users provide consent through browser setting[90]. Consent must be obtained through a clear, affirmative action by the user – who can reject all cookies, allow all cookies, or choose a setting in between.

ePrivacy Regulation, as originally proposed, has received a lot of (often justified) criticism from the digital advertising industry. As warned by IAB Europe, the law would undeniably damage the advertising business model – without achieving any real benefits for users from a privacy and data protection point of view[91]. The fear is that ePrivacy Regulation might enforce blocking of all, or at least third-party cookies in browsers by default. This would effectively disable cross-platform measurement and tracking, essential for providing advertising success metrics. Being unable to evaluate campaigns in the open digital advertising ecosystem, advertisers will shift budgets towards standalone platforms. With publishers resorting to paywalls, open and ad-financed journalism will be marginalized, and with that the dream of democratization of information will come to an end[92]. Naturally, blocking of third-party cookies in browsers by default would also be a major hit to the data ecosystem, vastly reducing the quantity, quality, and reach of available data.

Children's Online Privacy Protection Act (COPPA)

COPPA is a US federal law, regulating online collection of personal information of children under 13 years old. It applies not only to data collection on websites directed to children, but also via online services including mobile apps and general-audience websites – if they know they are collecting children's personal information[93].

Under COPPA, website operators are required to have a prominent privacy policy. A child's participation in a game, contest, or other activity cannot be based on the child's disclosing more personal information than is reasonably necessary to participate in the activity. They also need to obtain verifiable parental consent prior to collecting children's personal information, and allow parents to access, delete, and opt out of collecting such data. Confidentiality, security, and integrity of children's data must be maintained[94].

Health Insurance Portability and Accountability Act (HIPAA)

The Health Insurance Portability and Accountability Act regulates medical information. It can apply broadly to health care providers, data processors, pharmacies, and other entities that come into contact with medical information[95]. Among other provisions, the HIPAA requires a detailed privacy notice at the date of the first service delivery, and obtaining authorizations for the use and disclosure for certain purposes outside the scope of treatment, payment, and operations. Administrative, physical, and technical safeguards must be created to prevent unauthorized use or disclosure of private health information[96].

California Online Privacy Protection Act (CalOPPA)

The California Online Privacy Protection Act regulates collection of personally identifiable information of California residents. It applies to data collection both on website and online services, as well as via mobile apps. Personally identifiable information includes data such as name, address, phone number, Social Security number, or any other information that permits a specific individual to be contacted physically or online[97]. Under CalOPPA, a prominent privacy policy must be displayed[98]. Here, users can find out for example what PII categories are being collected, or which third parties might have access to the data.

In addition, CalOPPA also regulates visitor behavioral tracking across websites and mobile apps. Privacy policy has to state how the organization responds to "Do Not Track" signals from users' web browsers, or whether third parties may collect their personally identifiable information[99].

Digital Advertising Alliance (DAA) Self-Regulatory Program

The Digital Advertising Alliance is an independent non-profit organization led by leading advertising and marketing trade associations including American Association of Advertising Agencies (4A's), American Advertising Federation (AAF), Association of National Advertisers (ANA), Better Business Bureau (BBB), Data & Marketing Association (DMA), Interactive Advertising Bureau (IAB), and the Network Advertising Initiative (NAI)[100]. The DAA is in charge of a self-regulatory program (also known as AdChoices) focused on responsible privacy practices in the digital advertising ecosystem, with the aim of providing consumers with more transparency and control.

The DAA has issued self-regulatory principles for a number of areas[101] relevant to data usage in the digital advertising ecosystem. These include online behavioral advertising, multi-site data collection, mobile data collection, and cross-device data usage. The DAA is also behind the common arrow-shaped AdChoices icon[102] present alongside display ads, which directs users to a page with more information and an option to opt out of data-based targeting.

Chapter 8
Advertising data strategy

The quick rise of data-driven advertising in recent years presents a great opportunity and challenge for advertisers, agencies, and publishers. It is not easy to understand the ecosystem, make sense of it, and employ data in a way that would bring the highest return in the long run. In fact, designing and implementing a successful advertising data strategy is incredibly complex. Advertisers have at their disposal a broad range of data sources (first-party, second-party, and myriads of third-party providers), channels (open ecosystem and standalone platforms), and technologies. At the same time, they are restricted by applicable regulation, organization scale and maturity, and the overall business strategy of their organization. To make things even more difficult, the technology landscape and strategic context in general is constantly shifting. This chapter should serve as the first step for thinking about an advertising data strategy, and provide a simple framework to tie all the various aspects together. Let us begin with a basic question and work from there – what actually is an advertising data strategy?

Advertising data strategy is part of an organization's overall data strategy providing actionable vision for developing data-centered capability in digital advertising. This definition has several components worth discussing.

First of all, an advertising data strategy cannot exist in a vacuum – it must be aligned with an organization's data strategy, and in turn overall business strategy. Two basic approaches are possible – either data strategy informs business strategy, or vice versa. Data, with its enormous power, can enable new business models and disrupt established industries. A good example is Square, using data from payments processing to estimate risk of business loans better than any bank. Alternatively, data strategy can be designed to support an existing business strategy. In either case, advertising data strategy must be aligned with it.

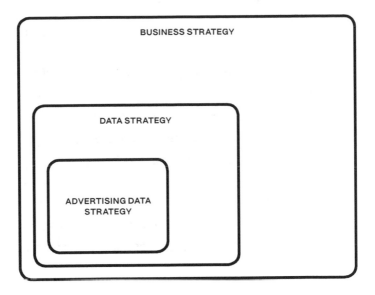

FIGURE 9: STRATEGIC ALIGNMENT

Secondly, a good advertising data strategy should provide an actionable vision. It has to be adequate for the organization in terms of skills and resources, but at the same time aspire to move things forward. For instance, a small business should not try to implement an advanced strategy centered around a data management platform. On the other hand, large organizations should not be content with fragmented and one-off usage of advertising data across isolated channels and campaigns, without building better customer understanding and increasing digital advertising ROI over time. Actionability also implies management buy-in – if the organization leadership is not on board, implementation will be difficult or impossible.

Finally, an advertising data strategy should be aimed at developing a valuable, strategic capability. If digital advertising is a key component of the business model, it needs to be supported by a solid data-centered capability in order to meet business objectives. This can only be achieved over time – the advertising data strategy cannot therefore be static, but must continually evolve.

Defining objectives

The first step in developing an advertising data strategy is clarification and definition of objectives, in line with broader data and business strategy. Objectives might include for example:

- Reaching new relevant target audiences
- Increasing digital campaign ROI
- Making dormant data assets actionable
- Improving operational workflow and reporting
- Opening a new revenue stream from selling advertising data

- Enhancing an existing advertising product with the use of data
- Data regulation compliance
- Individually tailoring communication/user experience
- Better understanding of converting and potential customers
- Building deep customer knowledge over time for effective one-on-one communication
- Developing special data asset/capability to support a unique business model

Each organization would have a different set of key objectives. It is best to focus on fewer objectives at first, but design the strategy in a way that can support all the required objectives over time.

Resources, available talent, and organization buy-in need to be considered as well – if the objectives are not actionable, advertising data strategy is useless. It is important to have a clear business case for each objective or set of objectives – otherwise the advertising data strategy might not be sustainable, and probably will not get management approval.

Advertising data strategy framework

Once the objectives for an advertising data strategy have been clarified, we can move on to designing the strategy itself. The following framework is a simple tool to guide thinking/discussions and provide basic structure. Three main components – Data Sources, Data Management, and Data Activation – are connected with arrows indicating a conceptual flow.

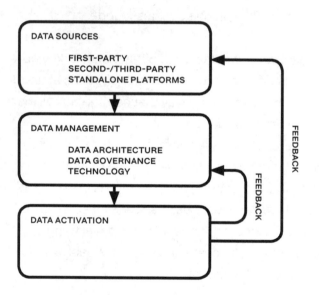

FIGURE 10: ADVERTISING DATA STRATEGY FRAMEWORK

Data sources

Data is the essential "raw material" an advertising data strategy works with in a given context. As mentioned in Chapter 1, data can be broadly categorized by ownership into first-party and external (second- and third-party).

First party data is the primary data resource that should be thoroughly explored, enhanced, and utilized. Many organizations already collect and use their first-party data. This includes website and mobile data, data from ad campaigns, data collected by analytics tools, CRM data, or email data. The main advantages include known origin (and hence quality), relevance, and very importantly no extra cost. A thorough audit of first-party data sources is necessary to determine if the organization is taking advantage of their full potential. Also, an audit might help make sure any data collection is carried out in a privacy-compliant manner.

With external data sources, things get a bit more complicated as options increase. Just like with first-party data, an audit of available external data sources should be conducted. There might be potential partners out there willing to share their data (at a cost, or even free in a data swap arrangement). Such second-party data is valuable, as it retains first-party data quality, while increasing reach or depth of our own data.

Third-party data options are the most complex. On the one hand, there is the open ecosystem with a broad selection of data vendors and exchanges. As noted earlier in this book, data selection is highly dependent on the market and technology platforms used. On the other hand, standalone advertising platforms offer their data for targeting more or less globally, but restrict some of the data flow.

With a good understanding of available data sources, we can take an educated guess at which of them would best fulfill our strategic objectives. It is not necessary to use all the data sources at our immediate disposal. Conversely, it is worth going the extra mile to acquire a data source that would be critical in successful implementation of the advertising data strategy. An initial data source selection is not set in stone, but should allow for dynamic changes once execution gets under way.

Data management

Data Management is the second component of the advertising data strategy framework. It is very broad, encompassing everything that happens between sourcing data and its activation. It defines basic data architecture, governance, and technologies. Let us look at all these aspects one by one.

Data architecture is the way in which information flows around the organization[103]. In other words, data architecture is the blueprint for getting data from its multiple sources to activation across all defined objectives. As the advertising data strategy is a subset of an organization's data strategy, advertising data architecture is likewise a subset of overall data architecture. In an ideal world, the two would be designed together, so the "piping" and standards work for both. However, sometimes the data strategy does not take into account advertising needs, making things difficult. A common advertising data architecture pattern for large organization is a DMP acting as a "data hub" – with raw data flowing in from various sources, and processed data flowing out to different activation platforms.

Data governance is the way practical control is exercised over the data flow, and involves defining processes, setting policies, and clarifying employee roles as they relate to data. It can be thought of as the formal definition of an organization's data culture. Two aspects are of particular importance when it comes to data governance – privacy and data security[104]. With the rise of privacy regulation, every organization handling user data needs to manage compliance, or face the risk of stiff penalties. Data security includes aspects such as data transfer, storage, or the anonymization or pseudonymization of personal data. GDPR requirements and guidelines are a good starting point for designing an organization's data governance.

Technology plays a significant role in the way data is managed. Chosen well, it enables and supports a desired data architecture and governance. When designing an advertising data strategy, it might be a good idea to leave thinking about specific technologies to a later stage of the process – only after objectives and an ideal data flow and control design has been determined. Technology should not unnecessarily limit strategic options. That said, a general understanding of technology landscape is necessary from the beginning, to keep strategic planning both realistic and confidently ambitious. Another consideration is whether to build any technologies in-house, or buy a solution from an external vendor[105]. Both options are valid, and each might be the better choice for a particular organization.

Data activation

Data Activation is where most of the strategic objectives are fulfilled. For example, if our objective was to reach relevant audiences, we can activate data for programmatic targeting through a demand-side platform. If we wanted to open a new revenue stream, we activate data by making it available for sale on a data exchange. Data activation is key, and must be aligned not only with objectives, but also with other components of the advertising data strategy framework – Data Sources and Data Management.

An important decision, particularly when it comes to data activation, is whether to outsource this activity. While it might be very convenient to leave activation (especially if it is mostly audience targeting) to an agency, caution is required. The agency must be absolutely aligned with our advertising data strategy in terms of objectives, data architecture, and governance. In addition, the collaboration must be set up in a way that would not hinder feedback from the real world.

Data activation is not the final point of data flow. It is the moment of truth and a valuable source of feedback and learning. Once activated, is advertising data meeting our objectives? How well? Can we improve? This is where feedback loops come into play.

Feedback loops

A good advertising data strategy should be designed with formalized feedback loops from the very beginning. This is the point where mere execution turns into a true capability through learning and constant optimization. In our schema, two primary feedback loops are indicated via conceptual flow arrows.

The first feedback loop exists between the point of activation and data management. Let us illustrate this with an example. Suppose there is an audience segment of fashion lovers, which we activated through a DSP. Now that we see initial campaign metrics, is there any way we can improve at the data management stage? Maybe a different audience definition would help, or perhaps the segment could be augmented with data from a different source. Could we run a look-a-like model to increase reach? If performance is great, what can we learn from this campaign and replicate in the future? This feedback loop can improve any of the three components (architecture, governance, technology). For instance, if technology turns out to be inadequate (e.g. data transfer too slow for efficient retargeting), maybe there is a need for change.

The second feedback loop goes a bit further – all the way to data sources. In the fashion lover scenario, data activation might show performance to be unacceptable to the point new data sources need to be explored. In a different example, a publisher might be selling data for additional revenue. The data activation stage could show a high demand for particular data or audience segments. This is valuable feedback, and the publisher can go back to their data sources to try and add similar segments or extend the existing ones. Again, this feedback loop serves to optimize the data strategy over time and enable learning in the process.

Developing an advertising data strategy

This section is intended as a guide for an internal discussion about advertising data strategy. Although such a project is often championed by a single lead, it might be a good idea to involve a broader team from the very beginning. This would not only help gain support for any changes, but will serve in building a data-first mindset and culture in the organization. An audit of existing technologies, processes, and learning will be useful prior to embarking on this exercise, to understand the organization's precise starting point.

Objectives and alignment

- What is our business strategy?
- What is our mission and vision?
- Which objectives do we want to achieve with our advertising data strategy?
- How well are they aligned with our business strategy?
- How well are they aligned with our data strategy?
- Is there a strong business case behind these objectives?
- Do these objectives provide a vision we can aspire to?

- Is our budget sufficient?
- Do we have the talent required for success-ful implementation?
- Is top management on board?
- Will these objectives help us develop a valu-able capability?

Data sources

- Which first-party data sources are available?
- Are there any (potential) partners with valu-able data?
- Which third-party data vendors operate in our region?
- What data is available on standalone adver-tising platforms in our region?
- How much would external data cost?
- Do we need a specific technology to access some data sources?
- Of all these data sources, which are likely to help us meet our objectives?

Data management

- How will data flow from its sources to activa-tion points?

- Which processes do we need to define to control this flow?
- Do we have a data policy?
- Which regulations does it need to comply with?
- Who will be responsible for advertising data management and compliance?
- Which user roles do we need to define in relation to advertising data?
- Do we need a data education program for employees?
- Which technologies/advertising platforms do we need to execute our strategy?
- How would new technologies fit within our current setup?
- Is there a strong business case for significant technology investments?

Data activation

- Which data activation points do we need to meet our objectives?
- Do we outsource any of them?
- Which technologies/technology platforms best meet our data activation needs?
- Are there any risks connected with data activation?

Feedback loop

- What do we need to measure for effective feedback?
- Which processes need to be defined for feedback to be actioned?
- Can we automate any of them (with the right technology)?
- Which feedback loops are critical for developing a strategic advertising data capability?
- Can we formalize the learning process?

Every organization is unique, so this list of questions should only serve as a guide for developing a custom one. Going through a process of finding answers to these questions will help design a well-thought-out strategy. Naturally, this is only the beginning. Next steps might include for example talking to technology and data vendors, running an RFP process, implementing a chosen solution, data and platform integrations, hiring qualified staff, and getting the organization aligned. It would go beyond the scope of this book to discuss these steps in detail, but plenty of tips and resources are available online. Also, nothing is set in stone – an advertising data strategy is more of a process than a static document, and should evolve over time as the organization matures.

Conclusion

Data usage in digital advertising is already revolutionizing the industry, and this trend is bound to accelerate. Several factors will play a key role in shaping it over the next few years, including automation, simplification, data control and privacy regulation, or the emergence/growth of new data sources.

Automation will gradually replace manual processes, particularly when it comes to media buying decisions, campaign optimization, and attribution. There is no question artificial intelligence can be better at running digital advertising campaigns than humans – in fact, it is the only way if they are to be truly personalized. For this to happen though, algorithms need to be fed data that is integrated across all sources, consolidated around an accurate ID graph, of high quality, timely, and complete (particularly when it comes to campaign/activation metrics measurement). These are not easy hurdles to overcome, and progress will be quicker in some areas than others.

Just like any revolution, things first get messy before a gradual simplification begins. There has been an explosion of advertising data-related sources, vendors, platforms, and technologies over the past few years. This is very hard to make sense of, let alone manage. At the same time, data flow can be extremely convoluted – making it inefficient (due to data losses between various systems) and hard to control from the data privacy and security perspective. Having too many vendors, both in the ecosystem as well as in individual advertisers' tech stacks, is not sustainable either. On the one hand, it leads to increasing complexity and "technology tax" (a proportion of digital advertising budget which is spent on enabling technologies, rather than media or data) for advertisers. On the other hand, fierce competition is putting pressure on vendors' profit margins. There is a universal demand for simplification, and it will arrive in time. Further industry consolidation is likely, with fewer full-stack advertising platforms (perhaps both open and standalone) dominating the space.

Data control will remain a critical battlefield. Direct relationship with customers (and in turn access to their data) will determine the winners and losers. Only players at the very source will be able to control (and restrict) data flow over the long term, and capture a lot of its value for themselves. This has happened with search data, and will happen universally. At the same time, individuals will rightly demand (and most probably get through regulation) more control over their personal data. This has already begun with the General Data Protection Regulation and other laws, and will likely continue into the future.

Finally, new data sources will play a big role going forward. Of these, voice search is especially interesting – it opens a whole new and very personal interface. The dominant player in voice search might get to control the bulk of customer relationships – not only with their own customers, but of many other companies. Depending on user adoption, voice search might have a profound impact on advertising data landscape. Other new data sources, such as virtual reality, wearables, or internet-of-things devices, are likely to bring unique and exciting data points into the ecosystem. User identification across platforms and their daily life, both online and offline, will likely improve as well – aided by initiatives like DigiTrust[106] (universal user token shared across the industry) or face recognition technology.

Advertising data is causing a revolution, which is already under way but still in the early stages. It is high time to start thinking about data from a long-term perspective, and develop a solid advertising data strategy. We might be closer to true one-on-one marketing than we think, and it would be a shame not to take advantage of this amazing opportunity.

About the author

Dominik Kosorin is the Managing Director at Ad Tech Research, a boutique research and advisory company specializing in programmatic advertising and data. He is the author of "Introduction to Programmatic Advertising." Dominik lives in Prague with a wonderful wife and an amazing son.

WEB:
WWW.ADTECHRESEARCH.COM

EMAIL:
DOMINIK.KOSORIN@ADTECHRESEARCH.COM

LINKEDIN:
WWW.LINKEDIN.COM/IN/DOMINIKKOSORIN

TWITTER:
@DKOSORIN

1   Kosorin, Dominik. Introduction to Programmatic Advertising. Charleston, SC, 2016.

2   Facebook Business: Marketing on Facebook. https://www.facebook.com/business

3   Facebook. "Facebook Reports Third Quarter 2017 Results.", Investor.fb.com, November 1, 2017. https://investor.fb.com/investor-news/press-release-details/2017/Facebook-Reports-Third-Quarter-2017-Results

4   Google AdWords – PPC Online Advertising to Reach Your Marketing Goals. https://adwords.google.com

5   Explore Amazon's advertising solutions – Amazon Advertising. https://advertising.amazon.com

6   United Parcel Service of America, Inc. "2017 UPS Pulse of the Online Shopperä Study." Solutions.upc.com, June 2017. https://solutions.ups.com/ups-pulse-of-the-online-shopper-LP.html

7   Molla, Rani. "Amazon could be responsible for nearly half of U.S. e-commerce sales in 2017." Recode.net, October 24, 2017. https://www.recode.net/2017/10/24/16534100/amazon-market-share-ebay-walmart-apple-ecommerce-sales-2017

8   Digiday. "Six ways Amazon will eat media and marketing." Digiday.com, 2017. https://digiday.com/amazonguide

9   Amazon Advertising Platform. https://advertising.amazon.com/amazon-advertising-platform

10   Amazon Marketing Services (AMS) – Advertise at Amazon. https://ams.amazon.com

11   Amazon Advertising Platform. https://advertising.amazon.com/amazon-advertising-platform

12   Digiday. "Six ways Amazon will eat media and marketing." Digiday.com, 2017. https://digiday.com/amazonguide

13   Amazon Marketing Services (AMS) – Advertise at Amazon. https://ams.amazon.com

14   Amazon Advertising blog. "Securely improve cross-channel campaign performance with Advertiser Audiences." Advertising.amazon.com, June 12, 2017. https://advertising.amazon.com/blog/advertiser-audiences

15   Twitter for Business: Twitter tips, tools and best practices. https://business.twitter.com

16   Twitter. "Q3 2017 Letter to Shareholders." Files.shareholder.com, October 26, 2017. http://files.shareholder.com/downloads/AMDA-2F526X/5458918398x0x961121/3D6E4631-9478-453F-A813-8DAB496307A1/Q3_17_Shareholder_Letter.pdf

17   Awan, Aatif. "The Power of LinkedIn's 500 Million Member Community." Blog.linkedin.com, April 24, 2017. https://blog.linkedin.com/2017/april/24/the-power-of-linkedins-500-million-community

18   LinkedIn Ads: Targeted Self-Service Ads. https://business.linkedin.com/marketing-solutions/ads

19   LinkedIn Help. "Targeting Options and Best Practices for LinkedIn Advertisements." Linkedin.com. https://www.linkedin.com/help/linkedin/answer/722

20   eBay Inc. "eBay Inc. Reports Third Quarter 2017 Results" Investors.ebayinc.com, October 18, 2017. https://investors.ebayinc.com/releasedetail.cfm?ReleaseID=1044445

21   eBay Advertising. http://www.ebayadvertising.com

22   eBay Inc. "Audience Buying Guide." Cc.ebay.com, 2016. http://cc.ebay.com/docs/default-source/documents/dmk/global-dmk/ebay-advertising_audience-guide_2016.pdf

23   Snapchat Ads. https://forbusiness.snapchat.com

24   Pinterest Ads. https://ads.pinterest.com

25   Martinson, Jane. "Pinterest chief Ben Silbermann: 'we're not a social network." Theguardian.com, June 12, 2016. https://www.theguardian.com/media/2016/jun/12/pinterest-ben-silbermann-social-network

26   Targeting. https://help.pinterest.com/en/articles/targeting

27   33Across. http://33across.com

28   Acxiom. www.acxiom.com

29   AffinityAnswers. www.affinityanswers.com

30   ALC Digital. www.alcdigital.com

31   Alliant Insight. http://alliantinsight.com

32   AnalyticsIQ. http://analytics-iq.com

33   Bombora. https://bombora.com

34   CACI. https://www.caci.co.uk

35   Cardlytics. http://www.cardlytics.com

36   comScore. www.comscore.com

37   Connexity. http://connexity.com

38   Cross Pixel. http://datadesk.
      crsspxl.com

39   Cuebiq. www.cuebiq.com

40   Experian. www.experian.com

41   Eyeota. http://www.eyeota.com

42   FinancialAudiences. http://
      financialaudiences.com

43   IRI. www.iriworldwide.com

44   Kantar Shopcom. http://www.
      kantarshopcom.com

45   iBehavior. www.i-behavior.com

46   Lotame. https://www.lotame.
      com

47   Mastercard Advisors. https://
      www.mastercardadvisors.com

48   Merkle Inc. https://www.
      merkleinc.com

49   Mobilewalla. www.mobilewalla.
      com

50   Navegg. https://www.navegg.
      com

51   Neustar, Inc. https://www.neus-
      tar.biz

52   The Nielsen Company (US), LLC.
      http://www.nielsen.com

53   OneAudience. http://www.
      oneaudience.com

54   Introduction to Oracle BlueKai
      Marketplace. https://docs.
      oracle.com/en/cloud/saas/
      data-cloud/dsmkt/introduc-
      tion-oracle-bluekai-market-
      place.html

55   PushSpring. http://pushspring.
      com

56   Retargetly. http://retargetly.
      com

57   Semasio GmbH. http://www.
      semasio.com

58   Skimlinks. https://skimlinks.com

59   TruSignal, Inc. https://www.
      tru-signal.com

60   V12 Data. http://www.v12data.
      com

61   Visa, Inc. https://usa.visa.com

62   VisualDNA. https://www.visu-
      aldna.com

63   Webbula, LLC. https://webbula.
      com

64   Ziff Davis, LLC. http://www.
      ziffdavis.com

65   Tableau. https://www.tableau.
      com

66   GoodData Corporation. https://
      www.gooddata.com

67   Screen6. https://s6.io

68   Tapad. https://www.tapad.com

69   Adform data management plat-
      form. http://site.adform.com/
      products/advertiser-edge/
      data-management-platform

70   Adobe Audience Manager.
      http://www.adobe.com/
      data-analytics-cloud/audi-
      ence-manager.html

71   The Adex data management
      platform. http://www.theadex.
      com

72   Amobee data management
      platform. https://www.amobee.
      com/platform/dmp

73   Google Audience Center 360.
      https://www.google.com/
      analytics/audience-center

74   Lotame data management plat-
      form. https://www.lotame.com

75   MediaMath data management
      platform. http://www.media-
      math.com/dmp

76   Neustar identity data manage-
      ment platform. https://www.
      marketing.neustar/identity-da-
      ta-management-platform

77   Oracle BlueKai data manage-
      ment platform. https://www.
      oracle.com/marketingcloud/
      products/data-manage-
      ment-platform/index.html

78   Salesforce data manage-
      ment platform. https://
      www.salesforce.com/
      products/marketing-cloud/
      data-management

79   Zipline data management plat-
      form. http://www.kbmg.com/
      products/zipline

80   DataSift. http://datasift.com

81   Kosorin, Dominik. Introduction
      to Programmatic Advertising.
      Charleston, SC, 2016.

82   Jolly, Ieuan. "Data protection
      in the United States: over-
      view." Thomsonreuters.com,
      July 1, 2017. https://uk.prac-
      ticallaw.thomsonreuters.
      com/6-502-0467

83   Interactive Advertising Bureau.
      "Digital Advertising Regulation
      101." Iab.com, February 3, 2014.
      https://www.iab.com/news/
      digital-advertising-regulation-101

84   Jolly, Ieuan. "Data protection
      in the United States: over-
      view." Thomsonreuters.com,
      July 1, 2017. https://uk.prac-
      ticallaw.thomsonreuters.
      com/6-502-0467

85   Jolly, Ieuan. "Data protection
      in the United States: over-
      view." Thomsonreuters.com,
      July 1, 2017. https://uk.prac-
      ticallaw.thomsonreuters.
      com/6-502-0467

86   Information
       Commissioner's Office. "GDPR
       Key definitions." Ico.org.uk,
       Accessed November 2017.
       https://ico.org.uk/for-organisa-
       tions/guide-to-the-general-da-
       ta-protection-regulation-gdpr/
       key-definitions

87   IAB Europe GDPR
       Implementation Working
       Group. "GDPR Compliance
       Primer." Iabeurope.eu,
       May 22, 2017. https://www.
       iabeurope.eu/wp-content/
       uploads/2017/06/20172205-IA-
       BEU-GIG-Working-Paper01_
       GDPR-Compliance-Primer.pdf

88   IAB Europe GDPR
       Implementation Working
       Group. "GDPR Compliance
       Primer." Iabeurope.eu,
       May 22, 2017. https://www.
       iabeurope.eu/wp-content/
       uploads/2017/06/20172205-IA-
       BEU-GIG-Working-Paper01_
       GDPR-Compliance-Primer.pdf

89   IAB Europe GDPR
       Implementation Working
       Group. "GDPR Compliance
       Primer." Iabeurope.eu,
       May 22, 2017. https://www.
       iabeurope.eu/wp-content/
       uploads/2017/06/20172205-IA-
       BEU-GIG-Working-Paper01_
       GDPR-Compliance-Primer.pdf

90   Venable LLP. "Summary of the
       Proposed ePrivacy Regulation."
       Iab.com, February 14, 2017.
       https://www.iab.com/news/
       summary-proposed-epriva-
       cy-regulation

91   The Interactive Advertising
       Bureau Europe. "IAB Europe
       Press release: Proposed ePriva-
       cy Regulation Fails To Improve
       Cookie Rules." Iabeurope.eu,
       January 10, 2017. https://www.
       iabeurope.eu/policy/press-re-
       lease-proposed-eprivacy-reg-
       ulation-fails-to-improve-cook-
       ie-rules

92   Schlosser, Jochen. "GDPR is
       great – no question about it! But,
       the newer ePrivacy Directive
       might be the end of the Internet
       as we know it." Linkedin.com,
       October 27, 2017. https://www.
       linkedin.com/pulse/epriva-
       cy-welcome-end-internet-jo-
       chen-schlosser

93   Interactive Advertising Bureau.
       "Digital Advertising Regulation
       101." Iab.com, February 3, 2014.
       https://www.iab.com/news/
       digital-advertising-regulation-101

94   Interactive Advertising Bureau.
       "Digital Advertising Regulation
       101." Iab.com, February 3, 2014.
       https://www.iab.com/news/
       digital-advertising-regulation-101

95   Jolly, Ieuan. "Data protection
       in the United States: over-
       view." Thomsonreuters.com,
       July 1, 2017. https://uk.prac-
       ticallaw.thomsonreuters.
       com/6-502-0467

96   Interactive Advertising Bureau. "Digital Advertising Regulation 101." Iab.com, February 3, 2014. https://www.iab.com/news/digital-advertising-regulation-101

97   Consumer Federation of California. "California Online Privacy Protection Act (CalOPPA)." Consumercal. org, July 29, 2015. https://consumercal.org/about-cfc/cfc-education-foundation/california-online-privacy-protection-act-caloppa-3

98   Interactive Advertising Bureau. "Digital Advertising Regulation 101." Iab.com, February 3, 2014. https://www.iab.com/news/digital-advertising-regulation-101

99   Consumer Federation of California. "California Online Privacy Protection Act (CalOPPA)." Consumercal. org, July 29, 2015. https://consumercal.org/about-cfc/cfc-education-foundation/california-online-privacy-protection-act-caloppa-3

100   Digital Advertising Alliance. http://digitaladvertisingalliance.org

101   Digital Advertising Alliance. "DAA Self-Regulatory Principles." Digitaladvertisingalliance.org. http://digitaladvertisingalliance.org/principles

102   YourAdChoices. http://youradchoices.com

103   Parkinson, John. "What is Data Architecture?" Linkedin.com, March 3, 2017. https://www.linkedin.com/pulse/what-data-architecture-john-parkinson/

104   Deloitte Digital. "Data Driven Marketing: How efficient and personalized customer dialog will work in future?" Deloitte.com, 2017. https://www2.deloitte.com/content/dam/Deloitte/de/Documents/technology/Data-Driven-Marketing-Whitepaper-Deloitte-Digital-2017-English.pdf

105   Deloitte Digital. "Data Driven Marketing: How efficient and personalized customer dialog will work in future?" Deloitte.com, 2017. https://www2.deloitte.com/content/dam/Deloitte/de/Documents/technology/Data-Driven-Marketing-Whitepaper-Deloitte-Digital-2017-English.pdf

106   DigiTrust. http://www.digitru.st